Boston Museum of Fine Arts, Henry F. Sewall, Sylvester Rosa
Koehler, S. R. Koehler

Exhibition of the Etched Work of Rembrandt

and of artists of his circle, together with engravings, etchings, etc., from

paintings and sketches by him

Boston Museum of Fine Arts, Henry F. Sewall, Sylvester Rosa Koehler, S. R. Koehler

Exhibition of the Etched Work of Rembrandt
and of artists of his circle, together with engravings, etchings, etc., from paintings and sketches by him

ISBN/EAN: 9783337127657

Printed in Europe, USA, Canada, Australia, Japan

Cover: Foto ©Thomas Meinert / pixelio.de

More available books at **www.hansebooks.com**

MUSEUM OF FINE ARTS.

PRINT DEPARTMENT.

EXHIBITION

OF

THE ETCHED WORK OF REMBRANDT,

AND OF ARTISTS OF HIS CIRCLE,

TOGETHER WITH ENGRAVINGS, ETCHINGS, ETC., FROM PAINTINGS
AND SKETCHES BY HIM. PRINCIPALLY FROM
THE COLLECTION OF

Mr. HENRY F. SEWALL,
OF NEW YORK.

APRIL 26 TO JUNE 30, 1887.

BOSTON:
PRINTED FOR THE MUSEUM BY ALFRED MUDGE & SON,
24 FRANKLIN STREET.
1887.

INTRODUCTION.

IT is now ten years since the Burlington Fine Arts Club, of London, opened (in May, 1877) its celebrated second exhibition of Rembrandt's etchings, — an exhibition which still holds a place in the memory of all who are interested in the great master, as a source of pleasure to those who were fortunate enough to see it, as a source of regret to those who were denied that advantage. The aim of this exhibition was twofold : Firstly, to afford to the visitor an insight into the development of the artist, to trace his progress step by step from early beginnings to the culmination of his powers ; secondly, to bring together the evidence needed to decide the question, to what extent Rembrandt's own work had been alloyed with that of others. It is easily seen that the first of these aims could only be reached by a chronological arrangement of the etchings executed by or attributed to Rembrandt. At the same time, the chronological arrangement would aid also in the attainment of the second aim, for in the sifting-out process, which must necessarily be one of comparison, a knowledge of the various stages passed through by the reputed author of all these works must self-evidently be of great importance. Mr. Francis Seymour Haden, the well-known etcher, took the principal part in the arrangement of the exhibition, as well as in the discussion which accompanied it. It was, indeed, his influence which shaped the exhibition in its essential features, and his theories regarding the authorship of the etchings in question were set forth at length in the introduction to the catalogue of the exhibition. That catalogue, owing to the exclusive policy of the Burlington Fine Arts Club, is unfortunately unobtainable, but the introduction was published by Mr. Haden as a pamphlet, both in English and in French.

The present exhibition has been arranged with a view
to furnishing to Rembrandt students in America similar, if
not the same, facilities which were furnished to these students in Europe by the London exhibition. But a somewhat difficult question presented itself at the outset. There
are two chronological lists of Rembrandt's work extant, —
an older by Mr. C. Vosmær, the author of " Rembrandt, sa
Vie et ses Œuvres "; a second, based upon the system
adopted at the exhibition of the London club, by Mr.
Charles Henry Middleton, author of "A Descriptive
Catalogue of the Etched Work of Rembrandt Van Rhyn."
Mr. Middleton's list is very precise, assigning each etching
to a distinct year, and thus very inviting as a clean-cut
piece of work, undisturbed by doubt or indecision. Mr.
Vosmær, on the other hand, often wavers and hesitates to
lay down his opinions as the law ; sometimes, indeed, pre-
fers to have no opinion at all. It was this comparative
modesty which finally commended his list. There is
something repelling in the audacity with which the author
of the " Descriptive Catalogue " assigns each print to its
particular year, and sometimes even undertakes to date the
various states, and, still more incomprehensibly, the
various parts of one and the same plate. Mr. Vosmær's
reasons for his decisions are, indeed, not always apparent ;
he is clearly in error sometimes, and occasionally he mis-
reads a date, but similar objections may also be urged
against Mr. Middleton. There is, moreover, this to be
said for Mr. Vosmær, that he leaves the student more
liberty of thought and of action than his English competi-
tor. Finally, by adhering to Mr. Vosmær's chronology,[1]
the exhibition becomes illustrative of his admirable

[1] As an additional help in fixing the presumable dates of Rembrandt's etchings, as well as in deciding the question of authenticity, the monograms, signatures, and figures found on the plates have
not as yet been taken fully into account. If that were the case, Mr.
Vosmær might, perhaps, have assigned some of the plates differently,
as for instance, " The Bathers," No. 35 of this catalogue, the signature
upon which certainly argues (as does also the work) for the later date.
It is a strange fact that the monograms on Rembrandt's earlier plates
have so far been misinterpreted by *all* cataloguers. Mr. Blanc prides
himself upon having discovered that many of these monograms read
RH (Rembrandt Harmenszoon), instead of *Rt* (Rembrandt), as in-

book on Rembrandt, or the latter may serve as a text-book for the exhibition, and this is an advantage not to be ignored.

As to Mr. Haden's theories concerning the authenticity of some of the plates attributed to Rembrandt, these can easily be tested by those desiring to do so by the aid of this exhibition, as a number of the plates by Van Vliet, Bol, and Lievens, mentioned by him in his " Monograph," are shown in it. How far these theories are sustained by the test, cannot be discussed here. Mr. Haden himself, in the prefatory " Note " to his second edition, admits that he has gone too far, or has at least ventured too much into detail as to the various etchers possibly involved. But it is clear that all the work which still goes under Rembrandt's name cannot be by him, or cannot now be in the condition in which he himself left it.

The desire to make the exhibition as complete as possible, to put the visitor in possession of as many as possible of the facts which he may need to enable him to arrive at an independent judgment, has led to the admission of a number of photogravure reproductions, not, indeed, in themselves very satisfactory, but still valuable as parts of a whole, where the originals themselves were not attainable. The proportion which these reproductions bear to the whole number of prints catalogued is, moreover, comparatively small.

The question as to what shape the catalogue should take, presented another difficulty. No doubt, for popular use, it would have been desirable to give explanations of the subjects, and biographical data concerning the persons represented, and to explain the differences which constitute

---

terpreted by earlier writers, and accordingly uses in most cases a combination of these letters, specially cut for his book, in the descriptions which he gives. But the monogram of this shape is of very rare occurrence on Rembrandt's etchings, the usual form being clearly a combination of *RHL*, in script. Dr. W. Bode (" Rembrandt's früheste Thätigkeit ") was the first to point this out, and to suggest the interpretation, " Rembrandt Harmenszoon Lugdunensis," — an interpretation which is borne out by the fact that this monogram disappears after Rembrandt's removal from Leyden to Amsterdam. In the present catalogue the monograms and signatures have been carefully noted, so far as that can be done without giving fac-similes.

the various "states." But that would have involved the reprinting bodily of some one of the older catalogues, or rather the construction of a new one from the materials furnished by the older, — obviously an impossibility for a variety of reasons, one of which it will be sufficient to state, to wit, the bulk and expense of such a catalogue. It was thought best, therefore, to give only such facts as are needed for an easy identification of each print, and the reference to the principal among the more extended catalogues. To these facts have only been added a few notes directing attention to the theories advanced touching the authenticity of some of the plates ; correcting obvious mistakes and supplying omissions in the recognized catalogues ; and occasionally expressing an opinion calculated to call upon the visitor to exercise his own independent judgment. For, in truth, the exercise of such judgment is sadly needed in this matter, which has been densely obscured by tradition and untrustworthy "authority." As it stands, the present pamphlet is a *Complete Short Catalogue of the Etched Work of Rembrandt*, according to Blanc and Vosmær, even those pieces having been enumerated in it which could not be shown, but which are mentioned by the writers named.

In the attempt to establish the "states" of the prints exhibited, Mr. Middleton has generally been followed, although he has been accused of unnecessarily multiplying states, and his book has been generally condemned (by Mr. Haden) as "disingenuous and unreliable." It, nevertheless, contains much that is not to be found in the older books, and is pretty closely adhered to, with occasional divergences, by Mr. Dutuit, in his luxurious Rembrandt catalogue, which is the latest work upon the subject. The tendency to unnecessarily multiply states is common to all catalogue makers, and the evils growing out of it are occasionally referred to in the notes in this catalogue. It must be acknowledged that the question of "states" is a difficult one, and yet a necessary evil, so long as prints are objects of commerce, and therefore of money value, and so long as the "connoisseur" of the ordinary kind is more of a curiosity hunter than an intelligent appreciator of art. It is to be hoped that in the good time coming, trial proofs will no longer be described as states, and press scratches and differences in printing will be recognized for what they are. Until then will it be in vain to look for really intelligible descriptions and for the absence of contradiction among the cataloguers, and until then, also, the ideal Rembrandt catalogue will have to remain unwritten. ·

It would seem almost as if, with the facilities for study and comparison now offered to the student, the advance must be rapid, and the settling of disputed questions could not be difficult. Books like those of Blanc and of Dutuit, and the reproductions by Amand-Durand (unfortunately not available in the preparation of this exhibition), are undoubtedly valuable, but for detailed study they are, nevertheless, unreliable. The photogravures in Blanc's book may, perhaps, claim to be reliable as far as they go, as they have been left unretouched, but for that very reason they are often uncouth to look at, and sin by omission. Besides, the process used, involving biting with acid (as far as known), is naturally liable to produce unlooked-for effects, and rudeness of line where it may be out of place. Such plates, on the other hand, as those in Dutuit's book, are more attractive to the eye, having been retouched. This, however, makes them still more unreliable (see No. 83, note, of this catalogue), and when it comes to the imitation of dry-point by roulette work, the distortion is complete. For the illustrated catalogue of the future, therefore, with purely practical aims, photogravure seems out of the question, and the simple photograph, at its best, much to be preferred. This catalogue of the future, furthermore, will have to aim at the reproduction of nothing but first states (*not* trial proofs, however), in contradistinction from Blanc's and even from Dutuit's catalogue, which in most cases reproduce late, and sometimes very late states.

The mention of states naturally enough brings up the inquiry as to the quality of the present exhibition. It may be admitted at the outset that it cannot rival the London exhibition in Hundred Guilders in the First State (see Mr. Haden's "Monograph," pp. 2 and 3), or Rembrandts with the Sabre ; that there are in it no Tholinxs (except in reproduction); no Buenos with the Black Ring (but a fine one with the white ring, see No. 244); no Old Harings and Turned-up Hats and Embroidered Mantles with "inestimable dates and *griffonnements*," — only the impressions usually met with, and many of them in late states. But there are in it, nevertheless, some fine impressions, and as to the states, it must be recollected that in some cases the earlier so-called states are really trial proofs, and that in many others they are almost unprocurable, so that, as has already been mentioned, even Blanc and Dutuit have had to content themselves with reproducing later states, and occasionally states later than those shown in this exhibition.

To students of various stages of progress and of various aims, the material offered to increase their knowledge is ample. Those curious about states, and the distinctions which constitute them, will find what they seek in Nos. 69, 83, 92, 102, 105, 107, 158, 163, 182, 209, 248, 251, 269, 276, 284, 285, 299, etc.; proof and counterproof may be compared in Nos. 86 and 225; the difference between an impression " showing plenty of bur," and another with the bur all gone, is especially well seen in No. 280 ; the deterioration of a plate by wearing may be observed in such examples as Nos. 114, 243, and 269. For technical study, nothing more attractive and instructive, and at the same time more difficult and puzzling, can be conceived of than an exhibition of Rembrandt's work. Never was there an artist better skilled, more audacious, and more successful in the use of all the means of which he had knowledge. Needle and acid, the dry-point, the graver, and the tricks of printing (except the modern device of *retroussage*) he used separately or in combination as he listed, and always with an harmonious and felicitous result. Even the graver (which, however, to speak quite correctly, he never used separately, but only for emphasizing and finishing), he handled with an unconventional freedom that made it match perfectly the unconcern of the point. (See some remarks on the use of this instrument by his followers under Nos. 454 and 464.) As examples of pure etching Nos. 210 and 260 may be pointed out ; pure dry-point work is seen in Nos. 165, 277, 299, 300, and probably also in No. 243 ; the combination of etched work and dry-point is

exemplified in such widely differing works as Nos. 263 and
269; in the production of No. 167 the graver has evidently had a share, together with the other means familiar
to the artist. But when it comes to such elaborate work
as No. 253, what shall we say? Did the acid do any of
the work? Or is it dry-point throughout, strengthened
here and there by the graver? Of the artifices in printing,
the exhibition shows nothing, except in Nos. 318 and (in a
manner too obvious to be attributable to Rembrandt himself) 103. To see some of the finest effects attained by
the artist by these means, American students are compelled,
for the present, to go to the collection of Mr. Theodore
Irwin, of Oswego, N. Y.

The main interest of the exhibition for the larger public
will be found, however, — and quite legitimately, — in
its autobiographical character. Rembrandt was born at
Leyden on July 15, 1607; he was buried Oct. 8, 1669, in
the Westerkerk at Amsterdam. The earliest date upon his
etchings is 1628, before he left Leyden; the last date found
on his plates is 1661. All his etched work embraced
within these dates is here, and the record is extended even
further by the engravings, etc., executed from his paintings
and sketches, which carry us from 1627, the earliest known
date upon any painting by him, to within one year of his
death. A survey of the exhibition makes it clearer than
any amount of reading could do it, that Rembrandt was
indeed the first artist who may truly be called modern.
For not only is he a realist of the realists, but what makes
him still more modern is his intense subjectivity.

It would be impossible, indeed, to bring together such
another exhibition, from the hands of another artist, offer-
ing a similar personal interest. Like the pages of an
autobiography, it lays bare to the attentive visitor every
step forward, every transformation of fortune, even the
varying moods of him who left it behind. Some of the
entries, no doubt, are enigmas; others are evidently fraud-
ulent interpolations, but enough of it is clear and intelligible, and authoritative beyond questioning, to tell the
story. And it is essentially a sad story, however instructive, — showing how even he, the great manipulator, began
timidly with the brush as well as with the point, — not

forgetting here the superb little portrait of his mother
(No. 4) which stands at the beginning as a prefiguration
of what was to come after, —and how the freedom of his
later years was the outcome only of the practice that went
before, — exhibiting him to us in the pride and triumph of
his youth, fond of show, ready to avail himself of the help
of others, rejoicing in the possession of Saskia, whose
radiant face smiles ever and anon upon us out of his work,
and then overwhelmed by misfortune, growing more sullen,
more sombre, more audacious, but still a giant in conception, and untiring of work, showing us, too, the place once
occupied by Saskia filled by the coarse woman who seems
to have been the companion of his later days, until we lose
sight of him altogether, and the light is quenched in dark-
ness. (See, however, Vosmær, pp. 358 and 372.)

It remains to give thanks to those who have made this
exhibition possible, first of all to Mr. Henry F. Sewall, of
New York, from whose rich collection — the richest in
Rembrandts, and the most complete, historically, of all the
private collections of the United States — by far the larger
part of the prints shown has been drawn. Acknowledg-
ments for assistance given are due also to Dr. H. C.
Ahlborn, of Boston, and Messrs. H. Wunderlich & Co.,
of New York (for the loan of Blanc's and Dutuit's works,
neither of which, unfortunately, is owned by the Museum),
to Mr. Chas. Henry Hart, of Philadelphia, to Mr. Edward
W. Hooper, of Cambridge, Mass., and to Mr. Edward
Robinson, of Boston.

The painting, " Danaë and Jupiter " (?), kindly lent by
Mr. Francis Brooks, forms an interesting supplement to
the exhibition. It is mentioned in no list of Rembrandt's
works, and Mr. Vosmær says : "I know of no painting
bearing the date of 1652." That is precisely the date upon
the canvas here shown. In its wealth of coloring it vividly
recalls the words used by Mr. Vosmær in describing another
picture by Rembrandt, " The Toilet of Bathseba," dated
1643 : "The harmony of the tints and of the general tone
is of great beauty. A color of bronze or of gold, inter-
woven with shades of violet, of brown, of green, and of
yellow ochre, envelops the whole in a scale at once warm,
poetical and mysterious." It appears to best advantage

in a strong light, thus bearing out Rembrandt's instructions concerning another of his works. " Hang this picture in a very strong light," he writes to Constantin Huijgens, under date of January 27, 1639, "and so that it can be seen at a distance. It will do best that way." The two copies of portraits form part of the collections of the Boston Athenæum, deposited with the Museum of Fine Arts.

S. R. KOEHLER,
Curator of the Print Dept.

As a text-book for the exhibition, Vosmær's *Rembrandt, sa Vie et ses Œuvres,* 2d ed., The Hague : 1877, is recommended.

Mr. Haden's theories will be found in *The Etched Work of Rembrandt. A Monograph,* new ed., London : 1879.

The catalogues referred to in this catalogue are :

Blanc, Charles, *L'Œuvre de Rembrandt,* 1 vol. and plates, Paris : 1880.

Bartsch, Adam, *Catalogue Raisonné de toutes les Estampes qui forment l'œuvre de Rembrandt,* etc. 2 vols., Vienna: 1797.

[Wilson, Thomas,] *A Descriptive Catalogue of the Prints of Rembrandt.* By an Amateur. London: 1836.

Middleton, Charles Henry, *A Descriptive Catalogue of the Etched Work of Rembrandt Van Rhyn.* London: 1878.

Dutuit, Eugène, *L'Œuvre Complet de Rembrandt.* 2 vols., supplement, and plates, Paris : 1883.

Claussin, Le Chevalier de, *Catalogue Raisonné de toutes les Estampe qui forment l'œuvre de Rembrandt,* etc., Paris : 1824. Supplement. Paris: 1828. (The supplement is referred to for the work of the artists belonging to Rembrandt's circle.)

For a short general account of etching in Holland under Rembrandt's influence, see S. R. Koehler, *Etching* (Chapter VI), New York: 1885.

To find in this exhibition any etching by Rembrandt, according to the numbers of Blanc, Bartsch, Wilson, Middleton or Dutuit, refer to the " Finding List " on p. 81.

The " Visitor's Guides," placed upon the stands in the First and Second Print Rooms, will be found convenient whenever it is desired to locate a special number in this catalogue in the cases.

The abbreviations used in the following pages hardly need an explanation : B. stands for Bartsch ; Bl. for Blanc ; Cl. for Claussin ; Du. for Dutuit ; M. for Middleton ; R. for Rembrandt ; V. for Vosmær ; W. for Wilson.

Right and left, when speaking of prints, are always understood as relating to the reader ; that is to say, right means that part of the print at his right hand, etc.

CONTENTS.

FIRST PRINT ROOM.

REMBRANDT'S ETCHINGS,

ARRANGED IN CHRONOLOGICAL ORDER ACCORDING TO C. VOSMAER'S LIST.

1. **St. Jerome in Meditation.** — Bl 77 ; B 149 ; W 147 ; M 176 ; Du 145. — Assigned to before 1628 by V., to 1629 by M.
One state only. Shown in photogravure. *From Bl.'s R.*

In his list V. places this print in the year 1629, but in the text of his " Rembrandt " (2d ed., p. 87) he gives it as his opinion that it and the following piece are anterior to the etchings of 1628.

2. **St. Jerome on his Knees.** — B 106 ; W 111 ; M 175. — Assigned to before 1628 by V., to 1629 by M.
One state only. *Not procurable.*

See remarks under No. 1.

3. **Rembrandt's Mother.** — Bl 192 ; B 352 ; W 347 ; M 6 ; Du 340. — Monogram *RHL.* Dated 1628.
Two states ; 2d state shown. *Sewall Coll.*

Two impressions are exhibited, the upper washed with India ink in the shadows. Most of the old women etched by R. are said to represent his mother, although there are certain considerations which argue against the assumption. The woman here represented must be from seventy to seventy-five years of age, and as R. was twenty-one years old in 1628, she must have been, taking it for granted that she was his mother, from fifty-one to fifty-four at the time of his birth and still older, of course, at the time of the birth of his younger sister Lijsbeth, which would certainly be phenomenal. It is said, moreover, that R.'s mother was about seventy at the time of her death in 1640 (Vosmaer, 2d ed., p. 202). It follows that in 1628 she was only about fifty-eight years old, which is altogether too young for the woman here represented. " R.'s Grandmother" would therefore be a more fitting title. His father's mother, who died in the year 1600, being out of the question, there remains only the conjecture that the woman represented may be his grandmother on the maternal side, Lijsbeth Cornelisdr.

4. **Rembrandt's Mother.** — Bl 193 ; B 354; W 348 ; M 5 ; Du 341. — Monogram *RHL.* Dated 1628.
Two states ; 2d state shown. *Sewall Coll.*

This magnificent little portrait which stands at the very threshhold of R.'s career as an etcher, adds an artistic enigma to the chronological riddle alluded to under No. 3. The woman represented might possibly be R.'s mother, but how is this etching, complete artistically and technically, to be reconciled with much of the later work which goes under the artist's name, such for instance as the heads No. 62 and No. 87? It seems impossible that the artist who did No. 3 should have done also, some years later, No. 62, No. 87 and their congeners.

5. **Head of a Woman.** — Bl 252 ; B 375 ; W 369 ; M 3 ; Du 363. — Assigned to 1628 by V. and by M.
One state only. Shown in photogravure. *From Bl.'s R.*

V. believes this also to be a portrait of R.'s mother, and a study for No. 4.

6. **The Presentation, with the Angel.** — Bl 24 ; B 51; W 56; M 178; Du 56. — Monogram *RHL* (the horizontal bar of the H omitted). Dated 1630.
Two states (?) ; 2d state shown.   · *Sewall Coll.*

M. describes only two states. An impression of a later state, not described, is in the Gray Collection.

7. **The Circumcision.** (Small, upright.) — Bl 21 ; B 48 ; W 53 ; M 179 ; Du 53. — Assigned to 1630 by V. and by M.
One state only. *Sewall Coll.*

8. **Jesus Disputing with the Doctors.** (Small, upright.) — Bl 37 ; B 66 ; W 70 ; M 177 ; Du 69. — The monogram and the date, 1630, in 1st and 2d states.
Three states ; 3d state shown. *Sewall Coll.*

9. **Two Beggars, Man and Woman,** coming from behind a bank. — Bl 129; B 165; W 162; M 10; Du 161. — Monogram in earlier states. Assigned to 1630 by V., to 1629 by M.
Seven states; 7th state shown. *Sewall Coll.*

10. **Two Beggars, Man and Woman,** conversing. —Bl 128; B 164; W 161; M 37; Du 160. — Monogram *RHL.* Dated 1630.
Two states; 2d state shown. *Sewall Coll.*

11. **A Beggar,** standing. — Bl 133; B 169; W 166; M 80; Du 165. — Marked RH IN, the letters of the name joined, but not in R.'s usual style. — Assigned to "early period" by V., to 1631 by M.
One state only. Shown in photogravure. *From Bl.'s R.*

M. is inclined to doubt this piece. According to him, it bears the monogram only, and he thinks there may be two states.

12. **A Beggar,** sitting on a hillock. — Bl 136; B 174; W 171; M 34; Du 170. — Monogram *RHL.* Dated 1630.
One state only? *Sewall Coll.*

13. **Man Standing.** — Bl 155; B 190; W 187; M 255; Du 187. — Monogram *RHL.* Dated 1630.
One state only. *Not shown.*

14. **Bust of a Man,** with broad-brimmed hat and ruff. — Bl 260; B 311; W 312; M 28; Du 307. — Monogram *RHL* (crossbar wanting). Dated 1630.
One state only? *Sewall Coll.*

There are impressions with and without monogram and date, these latter probably wiped out or covered up before the impressions were taken. The impression shown is of the second kind.

15. **Bust of a Man,** looking from behind a wall. — Bl 265; B 304; W 304; M 38; Du 300. — The 2d and 3d states have the monogram and are dated 1630.
Five states; two shown :—
(*a.*) 1st state shown in photogravure. *From Bl.'s R.*
(*b.*) 4th state. *Sewall Coll.*

M.'s description of the 1st state does not seem to be quite correct. According to him, the work on the 3d and later states is not by R.

16. **Old Man Sitting,** wearing a high cap (Philon, the Jew). — Bl 266; B 321; W 319; M 36; Du 314. — Monogram *RHL* (without the crossbar in the H). Dated 1630.
Three states; 2d state shown.   *Sewall Coll.*

17. **Bald Headed Man,** in profile, with a jewelled chain. — Bl 272; B 292; W 294; M 39; Du 289. — In 2d and 3d states, monogram *RHL*, and date, 1630.
Three states; 3d state shown.   *Sewall Coll.*

18. **Same as No. 17, Reversed.** — Bl 273; B. 293; W 308; M 41; Du 290. — Assigned to 1630 by V. and by M.
Two states; photogr. of 1st state shown.   *From Bl.'s R.*

19. **Same Head as No. 17, Smaller.** — Bl 274; B 294; W 295; M 40; Du 291. — Monogram *Rt.* Dated 1630.
One state only.   *Sewall Coll.*

20. **An Old Man,** with large beard, the shoulders rising above the ears. — Bl 282; B 325; W 323; M 30; Du 318. — Monogram *RHL.* Dated 1630.
One state only.   *Sewall Coll.*

There are impressions in which the monogram and date have been suppressed.

21. **An Old Man,** with large beard, the shoulders lower than the ears. — Bl 283; B 309; W 310; M 31; Du 305. — Monogram *RHL.* Dated 1630.
One state only.   *Sewall Coll.*

22. **An Old Man** with large beard, the right shoulder left white. — Bl 285; B 291; W 293; M 29; Du 288. — Assigned to 1630 by V. and by M.
One state only.   *Sewall Coll.*

23. **Rembrandt**, with fur cap and light dress. —
Bl 226; B 24; W 24; M 27; Du 24. — Monogram. Dated
1630.
Five states; 4th (or 5th?) state shown. *Sewall Coll.*

Monogram and date only partly visible in the impression shown.

24. **Rembrandt**, grimacing. — Bl 214; B 10; W 10;
M 23; Du 10. — Monogram and date, 1630, in 1st state.
Three states; two shown : —
   (*a.*)   2d state.   Cut down.   *Sewall Coll.*
   (*b.*)   3d state.   Washed with India ink in the head.
                                          Sewall Coll.

25. **Rembrandt**, with bushy hair and small white
collar. — Bl 204; B 1; W 1; M 51; Du 1. — Monogram
RHL (without the crossbar). Assigned to 1630 by V.,
to 1631 by M.
Two states; 2d state shown.   *Sewall Coll.*

26. **Rembrandt**, with haggard eyes. — Bl 217; B
320; W 33; M 24; Du 33. — Monogram *RHL*, and date,
hardly legible, but generally read 1630.
One state only.   *Sewall Coll.*

27. **Rembrandt**, laughing. — Bl 218; B 316; W 29;
M 25; Du 29. — Monogram *RHL.* Dated 1630.
Three states; 3d state shown.   *Sewall Coll.*

M. thinks that the retouches which the 3d state shows are not by R.
Mr. Haden ("Monograph," p. 14) speaks of a "distorted 2d state" by
Van Vliet.

28. **Rembrandt**, with open mouth. — Bl 219; B 13;
W 13; M 22; Du 13. — Monogram. Dated 1630.
Two states; 2d state shown.   *Sewall Coll.*

In the 2d state part of the monogram is lost by the reduction of the
plate. Only faint traces of it and of the date are visible in the impression shown.

29. Rembrandt, with a broad nose. — Bl 208 ; B 4 ; W 4 ; M 42 ; Du 4. — Assigned to 1630 by V., to 1631 by M.

Two states; photogr. of 2d state shown. *From Bl.'s R.*

30. Rembrandt, stooping. — Bl 209 ; B 5 ; W 5 ; M 19 ; Du 5. — Assigned to 1630 by V. and by M.

Three states ; photogr. of 3d state shown. *From Bl.'s R.*

31. Rembrandt, with curly hair, tufted. — Bl 205 ; B 27 ; W 27 ; M 26 ; Du 27. — Assigned to the earliest period by V. ; according to M., the monogram and the date **1630** can with difficulty be read in the lower margin.

One state only. Shown in photogravure. *From Bl.'s R.*

32. Diana Bathing. — Bl 165 ; B 201 ; W 198 ; M 258 ; Du 198. — Monogram *RHL. ft.* Assigned to 1631 by V. and by M.

One state only.   *Sewall Coll.*

33. Danaë and Jupiter. — Bl. 168 ; B 204 ; W 201 ; M 259 ; Du 201. — Monogram *RHL.* Assigned to 1631 by V. and by M.

Two states ; 2d state shown.   *Sewall Coll.*

34. A Beggar, without beard, in a large cloak. — Bl 114 ; B 150 ; W 148 ; M 71 ; Du 146. — Monogram RHL (shape of the letters quite different from that usually employed). Dated **1631.**

Five states ; 4th state shown.   *Sewall Coll.*

The changes in the later states, M. thinks, are not due to R.

35. The Bathers. — Bl 117 ; B 195 ; W 192 ; M 292 ; Du 192. — Signed *Rembrandt. f.* Dated **1631** ?

Two states ; 1st state shown.   *Sewall Coll.*

There are some scratches in the figure 3 of the date, which M. thinks constitute a correction of the year to 1651. The work and the signature both certainly seem to show the character of R.'s later years.

36. The Blind Fiddler. — Bl 91 ; B 138 ; W 138 ; M 78 ; Du 136. — Monogram *RHL.* Dated 1631.
Three states ; 3d state shown. *Sewall Coll.*

According to M., the shading which characterizes the last state was not executed by R.

37. The Little Polander. — Bl 108 ; B 142 ; W 142 ; M 79 ; Du 140. — Monogram *RHL* (without the crossbar). Dated 1631.
One state only. Shown in photogravure. *From Bl.'s R.*

38. The Dumb Beggar. (Lazarus Klap ; de Lazarusklap ; the Leper.) — Bl 138 ; B 171 ; W 168 ; M 72 ; Du 167. — Monogram RH (somewhat different from the usual form). Dated 1631.
Six states ; 3d state shown in photogravure. *From Bl.'s R.*

39. Woman Crouching. — Bl 156 ; B 191 ; W 188 ; M 257 ; Du 188. — Monogram *RHL.* Dated 1631.
Two states. *Not shown.*

40. A Beggar in a ragged cloak. — Bl 131 ; B 167 ; W 164 ; M 70 ; Du 163. — Monogram *RHL.* Dated 1631.
Three states ; 2d state shown. *Sewall Coll.*

Generally said to be " in the manner of Callot," without much warrant.

41. A Beggar with a crippled hand. — Bl 130 ; B 166 ; W 163 ; M 74 ; Du 162. — Assigned to 1631 by V. and by M.
Three states ? 2d state (?) shown in photogr. *From Bl.'s R.*

This, like No. 40, is also said to be " in the manner of Callot." M. describes three, Du. four states. The impression shown seems to reproduce Du.'s 4th state.

42. A Beggar Woman, with a leather bottle. — Bl 132 ; B 168 ; W 165 ; M 75 ; Du 164. — Assigned to 1631 by V. and by M.
Two states ; 2d state shown. *Sewall Coll.*

M. thinks this piece "somewhat doubtful."

43. Two Venetian Figures. — Bl 119; B 154; W 151; M 73; Du 150. — Monogram apparently *Rt.* Assigned to 1631 by V. and by M.
Two states; photogr. of 2d state shown.   *From Bl.'s R.*

It is difficult to say why these figures should be called "Venetian," unless for the reason that the cap of one of them resembles the cap of the Doges.

44. A Peasant with his hands behind him. — Bl 103; B 135; W 136; M 89; Du 134. — Monogram RHL. Dated **1631.**
Four states; 4th state shown.   *Sewall Coll.*

Mr. Haden (see "Monograph," p. 15) speaks of this plate as a "vile" copy by Van Vliet.

45. Bust of a Bald Man, leaning forward, mouth open. — Bl 275; B 298; W 298; M 56; Du 294.— RHL. Dated **1631.**
Three states; 3d state shown.   *Sewall Coll.*

"Very doubtful," according to. V.   M. thinks that after the 1st state the plate was worked upon by others.

46. Bust of a Bald Man, with large nose. — Bl 276; B 324; W 322; M 57; Du 317. — Monogram apparently RH. Dated **1631.**
Three states; 2d state shown.   *Gray Coll.*

47. An Old Woman, wearing a dark head dress with lappets. — Bl 245; B 355; W 349; M 67; Du 343. — Monogram· RH. Dated **1631.**
M. describes three, Bl., four states, but the descriptions do not indicate all the changes the plate has undergone.
    (*a.*)   Bl.'s 4th state, in photogravure.   *From Bl.'s R.*
    (*b.*)   Seems to be M.'s 3d state, but is evidently later than Bl.'s 4th.   *Sewall Coll.*
    (*c.*)   Shows some little ·additional work, and would, therefore, constitute a still later state.   *Sewall Coll.*

One of the earlier states, with considerably less work upon it, especially in the hood, is reproduced in Dutuit's book. The later retouches are supposed to be not by R. The example of this plate may serve to show the often unimportant character of the distinctions which mark "states."

48. **Bust of an Old Man,** with a long beard. — Bl 281 ; B 260 ; W 261 ; M 62 ; Du 276. — Monogram *RHL.* 1st state dated **1631.**
Two states; 2d state shown.   *Chas. Henry Hart.*

49. **Bust of a Man,** in profile, bearded, wearing a cap. — Bl 298 ; B 317 ; W 317 ; M 69 ; Du 312. — Monogram RH. Dated **1631.**
One state only. Shown in photogravure. *From Bl.'s R.*

" Very doubtful," according to M.

50. **An Old Man,** with large beard. — Bl 284 ; B 315 ; W 316 ; M 63 ; Du 311. — Monogram *RHL.* Dated **1631.**
Two states ; 2d state shown.   *Sewall Coll.*

51. **A Man with a Short Beard,** fur cap, and embroidered cloak. — Bl 267 ; B 263 ; W 265 ; M 77 ; Du 279. — Monogram *RHL.* Dated **1631.**
Four states ; 4th state shown.   *Sewall Coll.*

52. **Bust of an Elderly Man,** with a cap and robe of fur. — Bl 264 ; B 307 ; W 307 ; M 58 ; Du 303. — Monogram RH. Dated **1631.**
Three states ; 3d (?) state shown.   *Sewall Coll.*

The third state is coarsely reworked.

53. **A Beggar,** sitting in a chair. — Bl 124 ; B 160 ; W 157 ; M 76 ; Du 156. — Assigned to 1631 by V. and by M.
One state only. Shown in photogravure. *From Bl.'s R.*

There is something strongly suggestive of Dürer in the whole conception of this figure.

54. A Beggar, seated, with a dog by his side. — Bl
139 ; B 175 ; W 172 ; M 65 ; Du 171. — Monogram apparently Rt. Dated **1631.**
One state only.   Shown in photogravure. *From Bl.'s R.*

The head seems to be that of the model who sat also for the "St.
Paul in Prison," an early picture by R., dated 1627. See the etching
by Baldinger, "Zeitschrift für bildende Kunst," 1874, reproduced in
Bode, " R.'s früheste Thätigkeit," No. 362 of this catalogue.

55. Bust of an Old Man, in a high fur cap. — Bl
302 ; B 299 ; W 299 ; M 118 ; Du 295. — Assigned to 1631
by V., to 1635 by M.
One state only.   *Sewall Coll.*

56. Rembrandt's Mother, in a black dress. — Bl
195; B 349; W 344; M 53 ; Du 337. — Monogram *RHL*
(the crossbar of the H omitted).   Dated **1631.**
Two states ; 1st (?) state shown.   *Sewall Coll.*

M. supposes the age of the woman represented to be 63 or 65 years,
which seems too young. See the remarks under No. 3.

57. Rembrandt's Mother, with a black veil. — Bl
196; B 343; W 339; M 54; Du 332. — Monogram *RHL.*
ft. Assigned to 1631 by V. and by M.
Four states ; 2d state shown.   *Sewall Coll.*

58. Rembrandt's Mother, wearing a lace cap. — Bl
198; B 348 ; W 343 ; M 55; Du 336. — Monogram *RHL.*
Dated **1631.**
Three states; 3d state shown.   *Sewall Coll.*

59. Rembrandt, with broad hat and embroidered
mantle. — Bl 211 ; B 7 ; W 7 ; M 52 ; Du 7. — In 5th
state monogram *RHL* and date **1631**; in 8th state, *Rembrandt f.*
Nine states ; 8th state shown.   *Sewall Coll.*

M. considers the plate in its later states to have been worked upon
by other hands than those of R. The age of the person represented
again inspires doubt. In 1631 R. was twenty-four. This youth, de-
spite the down about the mouth, looks hardly more than eighteen or
twenty at the utmost. The curious may find Mr. Haden's opinion
of this plate, "Monograph," pp. 3 and 23.

60. **Rembrandt**, with a fur cap. — Bl 223; B 16; W 16; M 45; Du 16. — Monogram *RHL.* Dated **1631.**
Two states; 1st state shown. *Sewall Coll.*

61. **Rembrandt**, with squinting eyes and bushy hair. — Bl 220; B 25; W 25; M 49; Du 25. — Monogram and date, **1631,** in 1st and 2d states.
Three states; photogr. of 3d state shown. *From Bl.'s R.*

Only the 1st state, according to M., is entirely by R.

62. **Rembrandt**, with fur cape. — Bl 222; B 15; W 15; M 48; Du 15. — Monogram *RHL.* Dated **1631.**
Four states; two shown: —
   (*a.*) 1st state; in photogravure. *From Bl.'s R.*
   (*b.*) 4th state. *Sewall Coll.*

According to M., the changes after the 2d state are not due to R.'s hand. According to Mr. Haden, the plate is a "vile" copy by Van Vliet. (See "Monograph," p. 15.)

63. **Rembrandt**, with fur cap of unequal height. — Bl 225; B 14; W 14; M 44; Du 14. — Monogram RH. Dated **1631.**
Two states; 2d state shown. *Gray Coll.*

Reworked in the 2d state, according to M., by other hands than R.'s.

64. **Sketches**, with a so-called Head of Rembrandt. — Bl 238; B 370; W 364; M 82; Du 358. — Monogram *Rt.* Date read **1631** by V. and by M., **1651** by others.
One state only. Shown in photogravure. *From Bl.'s R.*

If 1631 is the correct date, the head cannot be R.'s. The work, so far as a reproduction admits of judgment, certainly looks more like that of a later period. M. would have it that part of it is of earlier, part of later date.

65. **Rembrandt**, with very small black eyes. — Bl 213; B 9; W 9; M 21; Du 9. — Assigned to 1631 by V., to 1630 by M.
One state only. Shown in photogravure. *From Bl.'s R.*

66. Rembrandt, in an oval. — Bl 215; B 12; W 12; M 16; Du 12. — Assigned to 1631 by V., to 1630 by M. Two states; 2d state shown in photogr.   *From Bl.'s R.*

67. Rembrandt, in an octagon. — Bl 221; B 336; W 31; M. 20; Du 31. — Monogram RH.   Assigned to 1631 by V., to 1630 by M.
One state only. Shown in photogravure.   *From Bl.'s R.*

68. Rembrandt, with a soft round cap. (" R. aux trois crocs.") — Bl 224; B 319; W 28; M 47; Du 28. — Assigned to 1631 by V. and by M.
Five states; two shown : —
    (*a.*)   3d state in photogravure.   *From Bl.'s R.*
    (*b.*)   4th state.   *Sewall Coll.*

Worked upon by some other artist, in M.'s opinion, in the 4th state and perhaps also in the 3d. Mr. Haden speaks of a "distorted 2d state " by Van Vliet.

69. The Resurrection of Lazarus. Large. — Bl 48; B 73; W 77; M 188; Du 79. — Marked: *RHL* (in monogram) *v. Ryn. f.* Assigned to 1632 by V., to 1633 by M.
Nine states, according to M ; eleven, according to Bl. Three shown : —
    (*a.*)   2d state in photogravure.   *From Bl.'s R.*
    (*b.*)   8th state.   *Sewall Coll.*
    (*c.*)   9th state (of M.; 11th of Blanc?). *Sewall Coll.*

M. is of opinion " that this piece is to a large extent the work of Van Vliet." Mr. Haden professes (" Monograph," p. 25) " a general distrust of the plate," but hesitates "to pronounce upon it," as to its probable author. In his opinion, also, "the *ordonnance* of the plate" is not R.'s. For similarity in composition, compare the drawing in the British Museum, dated 1630, reproduced in Bode, " R.'s früheste Thätigkeit," No. 367 of this catalogue.

70. The Body of Jesus carried to the Tomb. — Bl 60; B 84; W 89; M 217; Du 92. — Signed: *Rembrant* (*d* omitted). Assigned to 1632 by V., to 1645 by M.
One state only.   *Sewall Coll.*

71. **St. Jerome Praying.** — Bl 72; B 101; W 106;
M 183; Du 104. — Signed: *Rembrant. ft.* (*d* omitted).
Dated **1632.**
Three states; 3d state shown. *Sewall Coll.*

72. **The Ratkiller.** — Bl 95; B 121; W 125; M 261;
Du 122. — Monogram *RHL.* Dated **1632.**
Two states; 2d state shown. *Sewall Coll.*

73. **The Ratkiller.** — Bl 96; B 122; W 126; M 260
Du 123. — Assigned to 1632 by V. and by M.
One state only. Shown in photogravure. *From Bl.'s R.*

Called a study for No. 72. Ruined in the biting and abandoned.

74. **The Persian.** — Bl 105; B 152; W 150; M 91;
Du 148. — Monogram *RHL.* Dated **1632.**
Two states; 2d state shown. *Sewall Coll.*

75. **A Man on Horseback.** — Bl 106; B 139; W
139; M 4; Du 137. — Monogram apparently *RH*,
reversed. Assigned to between 1630 and 1634 by V., to
1628, among the first attempts of R., by M.
Two states; 2d state shown. *Sewall Coll.*

76. **Head of an Old Woman.** — Bl 246; B 360; W
354; Du 348. — Monogram RH. Assigned to 1632 by
V., rejected by M.
Two states described by W.; 2d state shown in photogr.
From Bl.'s R.

77. **Portrait of Coppenol,** the Calligrapher. (The
Little Coppenol.) — Bl 174; B 282; W 284; M 162; Du
257. — Assigned to about 1632 by V., to 1651 by M.
Six states; 3d state shown. *Sewall Coll.*

V. assigns this plate to about 1632, not only on the evidence of the
style of the work, " la gravure," but also on that of the age of the sit-
ter. As Coppenol was born in 1598, he was thirty-four years of age in
1632. He certainly looks much older in this portrait. Compare No.
319.

78. A Cottage with White Pales. — Bl 332 ; B 232 ; W 229 ; M 308 ; Du 229. — Signed *Rembrandt. f.*; 2d state dated **1632**, according to V., **1642**, according to M.
Two states; 2d state shown. *Sewall Coll.*

On the impression shown the date, hardly visible, looks more like 1642 than 1632. It has hardly any value, however, as it is evidently a later addition, probably by another hand. Moreover, the date 1642 would place this plate, which is probably the tamest of all of R.'s landscapes, into the same year with " The Three Trees," and later than much of his far more vigorous work of the same kind.

79. The Flight into Egypt. — Bl 25 ; B 52 ; W 57 ; M 184 ; Du 57. — Signed : *Rembrandt inventor et fecit.* Dated **1633.**
Two states; 1st state shown (late impression ?).
Sewall Coll.

" A very doubtful piece," according to M. According to Mr. Haden, it is probably by Bol, from a design by Lastman.

80. The Good Samaritan. — Bl 41 ; B 90 ; W 95 ; M 185 ; Du 75. — In 5th state : *Rembrandt inventor et fecit.* Dated **1633.**
Five states ; two shown : —
    (*a.*) 2d state, in photogravure.   *From Bl.'s R.*
    (*b.*) 5th state.   *Gray Coll.*

According to M., this plate was executed partly by some pupil of R., as was also the additional work in the later states. Mr. Haden ("Monograph," p. 26) thinks it entirely the work of a pupil, possibly Bol. Bl., although controverting Mr. Haden's opinion, likewise, in accord with others, puts a low estimate upon the plate. Longhi, the celebrated engraver, on the other hand, in his book on engraving, declares it to be his favorite among R.'s etchings.

81. The Descent from the Cross. Large plate. — Bl 56 ; B 81 ; W 83 ; M 186 ; Du 88. — Signed : *Rembrant. ft.* (*d* omitted). Dated **1633.**
Plate spoiled in the biting. Fragment only shown (photogravure), as given by Mr. Haden in his monograph, "The Etched Work of R." *M. of F. A.*

82. The Descent from the Cross. Large plate.
Second Version. — Bl 56 ; B 81 ; W 84 ; M 187 ; Du 88.
— Signed : *Rembrandt. f. cvm pryvl.* Dated 1633.
Four states ; two shown : —

(*a.*)	2d state.	*Gray Coll.*
(*b.*)	3d state.	*Sewall Coll.*

Evidently executed with the aid of a pupil, whom Mr. Haden
(" Monograph," p. 27) supposes to have been Lievens, an opinion
which M. combats.

83. Adverse Fortune. — Bl 81 ; B· 111 ; W 115 ; M
262 ; Du 112. — Signed : *Rembrandt f.* Dated 1633.
Three states ; 3d state shown in three impressions : —

(*a.*)	Without text on back.	*Gray Coll.*
(*b.*)	With text on back.	*Sewall Coll.*
(*c.*)	Without text on back.	*Sewall Coll.*

The 1st state, before the cutting of the plate, etc., is reproduced in
Dutuit's book, but one of the alleged distinctive marks of this state,
the failure of the acid in the shading between the wings of the half-
closed door on the left of the print, is lost in the reproduction. The
three impressions here shown as 3d states differ slightly. No trace
whatever of the full name, " Rembrandt," can be discovered (even
under the magnifying glass) on the side of the vessel on *a*, but an
abbreviation of the name, " Rembr.," has been added, apparently by
hand. The second impression *b*, with text on the back, corresponds to
the description ordinarily given of the 3d state. Impression *c* shows
some additional work in the shading between the wings of the door,
and would, therefore, strictly speaking, constitute a 4th state, although
it is in every way finer and more desirable than *b*, showing that the
paltry differences which generally constitute "states" are not always
to be relied upon as evidences of quality. — V. proposes a new title for
this plate, viz.: "The History of St. Paul" (see his " Rembrandt," 2d
ed., pp. 124 and 125). Messrs. Haden and Middleton think the plate
was etched by one of R.'s pupils, possibly Bol., and M. is of opinion
that "the print itself has very little merit." Bl., on the contrary, considers it "one of the happiest compositions of R."

84. Jan Cornelis Sylvius. — Bl 186 ; B 266 ; W
268 ; M 110 ; Du 268. — Signed : *Rembrandt.* Dated
1633. M. reads 1634,
One state only ? *Sewall Coll,*

85. **Rembrandt's Mother.**—Bl 191; B 351 ; W 346;
M 101 ; Du 339.—Signed: *Rembrandt. ft.* Dated 1633.
Three states ; 2d state shown.   *Gray Coll.*

86. **Rembrandt,** with a scarf around his neck. — Bl
229 ; B 17 ; W 17 ; M 99 ; Du 17. — Signed : *Rembrandt.
ft.* Dated 1633.
Three states ; 3d state shown : —
    (*a.*)   Proof.   *Sewall Coll.*
    (*b.*)   Counterproof.   *Sewall Coll.*

87. **Rembrandt,** in a fur cap and dark dress. — Bl
210; B 6 ; W 6 ; M 17 ; Du 6. — Assigned to 1633 by V.,
to 1630 by M.
Two states; 2d state shown.   *Sewall Coll.*

88. **Rembrandt,** with the bird of prey. — Bl 207 ; B
3 ; W 3 ; M 100; Du 3. — Assigned to between 1632 and
1634 by V., to 1633 by M.
Three states ; 2d state shown in photogr. *From Bl.'s R.*

Supposed to have been finished by some pupil, possibly Van Vliet,
according to Bl. Mr. Haden also points to Van Vliet as the possible
author of the plate.

89. **Rembrandt,** with bushy hair, and strongly shaded.
— Bl 227 ; B 332 ; W 34; M 43 ; Du 34. — Assigned to
1633 by V., to 1631 by M.
Two states; 1st state shown in photogr. *From Bl.'s R.*

"Very doubtful," according to V. The monogram, *Rt* (although
the *t* might be a small capital *L*), seems to appear only in the second
state, reproduced by Dutuit.

90. **Joseph and Potiphar's Wife.** — Bl 11 ; B 39 ;
W 43 ; M 192 ; Du 43. — Signed : *Rembrandt. ft.* Dated
1634.
Two states.   *Not shown.*

91. **The Angel appearing to the Shepherds.** —
Bl 17 ; B 44 ; W 49 ; M 191 ; Du 49. — Signed : *Rem-
brandt. ft.* Dated 1634.
Three states ; 3d state shown.   *Gray Coll.*

92. The Samaritan Woman at the Ruins. — Bl 46; B 71; W 75; M 195; Du 73. — Signed: *Rembrandt. f.* Dated **1634.**

Two states (according to M.): —

    (*a.*) 2d state (with the scratch in the foreground).

                                      Gray Coll.

    (*b.*) 2d state (without the scratch).   *Sewall Coll.*

Bl. says that the description of the states of this plate has hitherto been unreliable, but that the three states described by him, according to Weber, settle the question. M. refuses to recognize the three states and allows only two. In spite of all this, however, it is still a difficult matter to determine the states, from the descriptions given. Impression *a* would seem to be M.'s 2d state, as it has the diagonal scratch in the white part of the foreground, etc. In impression *b*, on the other hand, — evidently in all essentials the same state, — this scratch is not seen, and there is also noticeable a difference in the shading over the left foot of Jesus. It is curious that a writer like Bl., with his practical knowledge, should place any reliance upon such marks, for a little experience at the printing press is sufficient to show their unreliability. A scratch on the copper may result from a particle of hard matter in the rag, and may show in a number of impressions, until the printer discovering it, it is removed by him with a touch of the burnisher. Much more interesting is it to note the evident influence of Rubens in the figure of Jesus, not only in the head, but in the whole of the pose. According to Mr. Haden, Gerard Dow is the reputed author of the composition of this plate.

93. Jesus and the Disciples at Emmaus. (The small plate.) — Bl 62; B 88; W 93; M 194; Du 95. — Signed: *Rembrandt ft.* Dated **1634.**

One state only.   *Sewall Coll.*

Although M. allows only one state, he nevertheless says that "the plate was coarsely retouched at some later time." The influence of Rubens is again very apparent in this etching, more especially in the figure of Jesus.

94. St. Jerome, reading at the foot of a tree. — Bl 71; B 100; W 105; M 190; Du 103. — Signed: *Rembrandt. f.* Dated **1634.**

Two states; 2d state shown.   *Sewall Coll.*

V., following the usual reading, makes the date (which can be read only with difficulty) 1654. But it is evidently 1634 in consonance with the character of the work, which is that of R.'s earlier period. M. thinks he sees the hand of Bol in parts of the plate. Mr. Haden also is inclined to attribute it to Bol,

95. **A Beggar.** "'tis vinnich hout."—Bl 140; B 177; W 174; M 112; Du 173.—Signed: *Rembrand* (no *t*, there being no room on the plate for it) *f.* (under the name). Dated **1634**.
One state only. *Sewall Coll.*

96. **A Beggar.** "Dats niet."—Bl 141; B 178; W 175; M 113; Du 174.—Signed and dated: *Rembran f* 163, in two lines, the last letters of the name and the last figure of the date wanting, there being no room for them. Assigned to 1634 by V. and by M.
One state only. *Sewall Coll.*

These companion pieces represent peasants rather than beggars. The last word in the legend on No. 95 is always given as *k*out, but it is clearly *h*out. According to Mr. Haden, "Rembrandt copied" these two plates from Hans Sebald Beham, and "Savry etched" them. To show how closely R. "copied", Beham's engravings, in faithful reproductions, have been placed alongside of the etchings.

97. **Woman seated** with hair let down. (The Great Jewish Bride.) — Bl 199; B 340; W 337; M 108; Du 329.—Signed: *R* (reversed). Dated **1634**.
Four states; 4th state shown. *Sewall Coll.*

This etching has also been called "Saskia," which is simply a libel upon Rembrandt and his charming first wife. If the plate were rejected, that would seem more natural. Even the more preferable 1st state, reproduced by Dutuit, is unworthy of its proposed new title and of its reputed authorship.

98. **Supposed study for No. 97.**— Bl 239; B 341; Du 330. — Assigned to 1634 by V., rejected by M.
Two states (?); 2d state shown. *Sewall Coll.*

V. and Bl. both doubt this plate. W., like M., rejects it.

99. **A Young Woman** reading. — Bl 242; B 345; W 341; M 109; Du 334. — Signed: *Rembrandt. f.* Dated **1634**.
Three states; 3d (?) state shown. *Sewall Coll.*

100. **A Young Woman** with pearls in her hair. —
Bl 201 ; B 347 ; W 342 ; M 107 ; Du 335. — Signed :
Rembrandt. f. Dated 1634.
One state only. *Sewall Coll.*

<small>This has also been called a portrait of Saskia, R.'s first wife.</small>

101. **Rembrandt,** with moustaches and small beard.
— Bl 206 ; B 2 ; W 2 ; M 106 ; Du 2. — Assigned to
between 1632 and 1634 by V., to 1634 by M.
Two states ; 2d state shown. *Sewall Coll.*

102. **Rembrandt,** with bushy hair. — Bl 212 ; B 8 ; W
8 ; M 50 ; Du 8. — Assigned to 1634 by V., to 1631 by M.
Six states ; three shown : —
    (*a.*) 1st state in photogravure. *From Bl.'s R.*
    (*b.*) 4th state. *Gray Coll.*
    (*c.*) 5th state. *Sewall Coll.*

<small>M. assumes that the additional work on the 3d and 4th states is by
R.'s pupils. That on the 5th and 6th states, according to the same
writer, is supposed to belong to a much later time. Mr. Haden speaks
of this plate as a "vile copy" by Van Vliet.</small>

103. **Head of Rembrandt** and other sketches. — Bl
237 ; B 363 ; W 357 ; M 136 ; Du 351. — Assigned to
about 1634 by V., to 1639 by M.
Three states ; 2d state shown in two impressions : —
    (*a.*) A heavy tint left upon the plate, parts only
           wiped clean with the finger. *Sewall Coll.*
    (*b.*) Wiped clean. *Sewall Coll.*

104. **Rembrandt** with a flamboyant sword. — Bl
231 ; B 18 ; W 18 ; M 105 ; Du 18. — Signed : *Rembrandt. f.* Dated 1634.
Three states ; 3d state shown. *Sewall Coll.*

105. **Rembrandt** with a sword, wearing a tufted cap.
— Bl 232 ; B 23 ; W 23 ; M 111 ; Du 23. — Signed : *Rembrandt ft.* Dated 1634.
Four states ; three shown : —
    (*a.*) 1st state in photogravure. *From Bl.'s R.*
    (*b.*) 2d state in photogravure. *From Du.'s R.*
    (*c.*) 3d state. *Sewall Coll.*

The recklessness and lack of judgment with which R.'s name has been connected with the male heads etched by or attributed to him, are easily seen upon a comparison of Nos. 104 and 105. M. calls the latter a " Portrait, Unknown." V. thinks it rather a study from R.'s figure than a portrait. But the face certainly has a marked individuality, and the mole at the right of the nose would hardly be in place in an ideal head.

106. The Landscape with the Cow (Ruins on the Seashore). — Bl 309 ; B 206 ; W 203 ; Du 203. — Monogram *RHL. f.* Dated 1634. V. thinks, however, that the date has been added by hand. Rejected by M.

Two states ; 2d state shown in photogr. *From Bl.'s R.*

107. Jesus Driving the Money Changers from the Temple. — Bl 44 ; B 69 ; W 73 ; M 198 ; Du 80. — Signed : *Rembrandt. ft.* Dated 1635.

Two states ; both shown : —

(*a.*) 1st state. .		*Sewall Coll.*
(*b.*) 2d state.		*Sewall Coll.*

The difference between the two " states " of this plate shows plainly the puerile character of many of the distinctions involved. M.'s order of states, which is the usual order, has here been followed, although Bl., who inverts it, is no doubt correct. There do not, in fact, exist two states. The dark spots around the mouth and on the forehead and sole of the man under the ox are due evidently to an accident, and were burnished out or disappeared of themselves, after a number of impressions had been taken. They are, therefore, evidences of priority rather than otherwise. The figure of Christ, it is well known, is a reversed copy of a figure in Dürer's Little Passion.

108. The Tribute Money. — Bl 42 ; B 68 ; W 72 ; M 196 ; Du 81. — Assigned to 1635 by V., to 1634 by M. One state only. · *Sewall Coll.*

Three states are usually described, but according to M., there is practically only one state.

109. The Martrydom of St. Stephen. — Bl 68 ; B 97 ; W 102 ; M 197 ; Du 100. — Signed : *Rembrandt. ft.* Dated 1635.

One state only. *Gray Coll.*

Two states are usually described, but according to M., there is practically only one state, although he admits that there are impressions from the plate after it had been "coarsely reworked."

110. St. Jerome Kneeling. — Bl 73; B 102; W 107; M 199; Du 105. — Signed: *Rembrandt f.* Dated **1635.**
One state only.   *Sewall Coll.*

111. The Mountebank. — Bl 92; B 129; W 132; M 117; Du 129. — Signed: *Rembrandt ft.* Dated **1635.**
One state only.   *Sewall Coll.*

112. The Pancake Woman. — Bl 93; B 124; W 128; M 264; Du 125. — Signed: *Rembrandt. ft.* Dated **1635.**
Four states; 3d state shown.   *Sewall Coll.*

113. A Nude Woman, sitting on a hillock. — Bl 162; B 198; W 195; M 256; Du 195. — Assigned to 1635 by V., to 1631 by M.
One state only.   *Sewall Coll.*

114. Johannes Uytenbogaert. — Bl 190; B 279; W 281; M 114; Du 272. — Signed and dated in 3d state: *Rembrandt. f.* **1635.**
Five states; two shown: —
    (*a.*)   3d state in photogravure.   *Sewall Coll.*
    (*b.*)   5th state.   *Sewall Coll.*
    (*c.*)   5th state.   *Sewall Coll.*

The signature does not appear to be by R. himself. The *b*, the *d*, and the *f* of the *fecit* are quite different from the form of these letters usually employed by him. Two impressions of the 5th state are exhibited, to show difference in printing and condition of plate.

115. Oriental Head. Full face. (Jacob Cats.) — Bl 173; B 286; W 288; M 122; Du 283. — Signed: *Rembrandt.* Dated **1635.**
Two states; 2d state shown.   *Sewall Coll.*

The assumption that this is a portrait of Cats, the poet, has been disproved by V. See No. 117.

116. Oriental Head. Profile, to right. — Bl 289; B 288; W 290; M 124; Du 285. — Signed: *Rembrandt.* Dated **1635.**
One state only. Shown in photogravure. *From Bl.'s R.*

The signature does not look like R.'s. See No. 117.

117. Oriental Head. Profile, to left. — Bl 288; B 287; W 289; M 123; Du 284. — Signed: *Rembrandt.* Assigned to 1635 by V. and by M.
One state only. *Sewall Coll.*

Upon the three etchings catalogued under Nos. 115-117 appears the mysterious word which has been read *Venetiis* and *renetus*, but which, according to V., reads *geretuckerdt*, that is to say, *retouched.* It is likely, therefore, that these plates are the work of a pupil, retouched by R. The signatures on Nos. 116 and 117 have peculiarities which plainly distinguish them from other signatures usually considered genuine. Mr. Haden's opinion of these plates can be read on p. 28 of his " Monograph."

118. The Crucifixion. Small plate. — Bl 55; B 80; W 86; M 193; Du 87. — Signed: *Rembrandt f.* Assigned to between 1630 and 1635 by V., to 1634 by M.
One state only. *Sewall Coll.*

Three states are usually described, but according to M., there is only one. The signature, which is very faint, hardly looks like R.'s.

119. The Travelling Musicians. — Bl 90; B 119; W 123; M 263; Du 120. — Assigned to between 1630 and 1635 by V., to 1635 by M.
Two states; 2d state shown. *Sewall Coll.*

120. St. Peter Healing the Cripple. — Bl 65; B 95; W 99; M 249; Du 98. — Assigned to between 1630 and 1635 by V., to 1655 by M.
One state only. Shown in photogravure. *From Bl.'s R.*

121. A Polander, turned towards the right. — Bl 107; B 140; W 140; M 102; Du 138. — Assigned to between 1630 and 1635 by V., to 1633 by M.
Two states; 2d state shown. *Sewall Coll.*

122. A Polander, with sabre and stick. — Bl 118; B 141; W 141; M 93; Du 139. — Assigned to between 1630 and 1635 by V., to 1632 by M.

Six states; two shown : —
(*a*.)   1st state.   Shown in photogr.   *From Bl.'s R.*
(*b*.)   5th state.   *Sewall Coll.*

M. thinks that the additional work after the fourth state is not by R.

123. An Old Man with a bushy beard. — Bl 115; B 151; W 149; M 32; Du 147. — Monogram *RHL*, reversed.   Assigned to between 1630 and 1635 by V., to 1630 by M.

Two states; 2d state shown.   *Sewall Coll.*

124. The White Negress. — Bl 241; B 357; W 351; Du 345. — Reversed monogram on first state.   Assigned to between 1630 and 1635 by V., rejected by M.

Two states; 2d state shown.   *Sewall Coll.*

125. A Young Man in a mezetin cap. — Bl 255; B 289; W 291; M 125; Du 286. — Monogram, apparently *RHL*, but only partly visible.   Assigned to between 1630 and 1635 by V., to 1635 by M.

Two states; 2d state shown.   *Sewall Coll.*

126. Bust of a Man, with a ruff, and feathers in his hat. — Bl 261; B 335; W 331; M 2; Du 326. — Placed by V. among the pieces assigned to between 1630 and 1635; assigned to 1628 by M.

Two states; 1st state shown in photogr. *From Bl.'s R.*

Of all the ridiculous things attributed to R., this little head is the most ridiculous. V. does, indeed, consider it doubtful, but places it as stated, probably on the strength of a scratch in the background which looks like a 5. Bl., M., and Du. accept it without qualification, and M. places it second on his chronological list, in close proximity to the admirable portrait, No. 4, of this catalogue.

127. An Old Man, in profile, with a short beard. — Bl 294; B 306; W 306; M 120; Du 302. — Assigned to between 1630 and 1635 by V., to 1635 by M.

Two states; 2d state shown.   *Sewall Coll.*

128.   Sketches of figures, divided by a line.— Bl 123; B 373; W 367; M 1; Du 361. — Assigned to between 1630 and 1635 by V., to 1628 by M.
One state only.   Shown in photogravure.   *From Bl.'s R.*

M. sees in these sketches R.'s first attempt at etching.

129.   A Beggar, warming his hands.— Bl 135; B 173; W 170; M 14; Du 169. — Assigned to between 1630 and 1635 by V., to 1629 by M.
Two states; 2d state shown.   *Sewall Coll.*

130.   A Grotesque Head in a high fur cap.— Bl 301; B 326; W 324; M 98; Du 319. — Assigned to between 1630 and 1635 by V., to 1632 by M.
Four states; two shown : —
   (*a.*)   3d state (?) in photogravure.   *From Bl.'s R.*
   (*b.*)   4th state (?).   *Sewall Coll.*

M.'s description does not fit the impressions shown, nor does it correspond with Bl.'s.

131.   An Old Man, in an ample velvet cloak and with a fur cap. — Bl 270; B 262; W 264; M 90; Du 278. — Monogram *RHL ft.*   Assigned to between 1630 and 1635 by V., to 1632 by M.
Three states; 2d state shown.   *Sewall Coll.*

132.   An Old Man, with a turned-up cap (in the 2d state). — Bl 280; B 337; W 332; M 96; Du 327. — Assigned to between 1630 and 1635 by V., to 1632 by M.
Three states; 3d state shown in photogr.   *From Bl.'s R.*

133.   An Old Woman, asleep over her book.— Bl 244; B 350; W 345; M 116; Du 338. — Assigned to about 1635 by V., to 1635 by M.
One state only.   *Sewall Coll.*

134. **Head of a Man** crying out. — Bl 299; B 327; W 325; M 97; Du 320. — Assigned to between 1630 and 1635 by V., to 1632 by M.
Two states; both shown : —

(*a*.) 1st state.	*Sewall Coll.*
(*b*.) 2d state.	*Sewall Coll.*

135. **Sketches** of five heads and a half-length figure. — Bl 308; B 366; W 360; M 83; Dü 354. — Monogram *RHL*, reversed. Assigned to between 1630 and 1635 by V., to 1631 by M.
Two states; 1st state shown in photogr. *From Bl.'s R.*
The plate was afterwards cut into five pieces. See Nos. 136 to 140.

136. **Bust of an Old Man,** in profile to right. (Part of No. 135.) — Bl 290; B 334; W 330; M 84; Du 325.
Two states; 2d state shown in photogr. *From Bl.'s R.*

137. **Bust of an Old Man,** and head of a cat. (Part of No. 135.) — Bl 292; B 333; W 329; M 85; Du 324.
Five states ; 2d state shown in photogr. *From Bl.'s R.*

138. **An Old Man,** seen from behind. (Part of No. 135.) Bl 109; B 143; W 143; M 86; Du 141.
Four states ; two shown : —

(*a*.) 2d state.	*Sewall Coll.*
(*b*.) 4th state.	*Sewall Coll.*

M. thinks the work on the 4th state due to a later hand.

139. **A Turkish Slave.** (Part of No. 135.) — Bl 293; B 303; W 303; M 87; Du 299.
Two states ; 2d state shown in photogr. *From Bl.'s R.*

140. **Bust of a Man,** crying out, turned to the left. (Part of No. 135.) — Bl 291; B 300; W 300; M 88; Du 296.
Five states ; two shown : —

(*a*.) 2d state in photogravure.	*From Bl.'s R.*
(*b*.) 5th state.	*Sewall Coll.*

According to M. the variations in the 3d and later states were not made by R.

141. **The Haycart.** — Bl 345; B 251; W 247; Du 248. — Assigned to between 1630 and 1635 by V., rejected by M.
Two states; 1st state shown in photogr. *From Bl.'s R.*

142. **Sketch of a Dog.** — Bl 351; B 371; W 365; M 266; Du 359. — Assigned to between 1630 and 1635 by V., to 1640 by M.
One state only. Shown in photogravure. *From Bl.'s R.*

143. **The Return of the Prodigal.** — Bl 43; B 91; W 96; M 201; Du 76. — Signed: *Rembrandt f.* Dated 1636.
One state only. .   *Sewall Coll.*

The composition of this plate is said to be by Heemskirk.

144. **The Ecce Homo.** — Bl 52; B 77; W 82; M 200; Du 84. — Marked in 3d state, with the graver, quite lightly and very clumsily: *Rembrandt ft. 1636. cvm privileg.*
Five states; two shown : —
    (*a.*)   3d state.   *Gray Coll.*
    (*b.*)   4th state.   *Sewall Coll.*

Mr. Haden in his " Monograph " gives a reproduction of a part of the unfinished 1st state, showing the engraver-like manner in which the work was done. The plate was probably executed, partly at least, by Lievens or Van Vliet. To the copies described by M. must be added another, rather effective as a whole, although very mediocre in detail; etched surface, h.–.537, b.–.444; marked *Rembrandt f.* in a clear space below. An impression in the Museum of Fine Arts.

145. **Landscape with a Flock of Sheep.** Arched. — Bl 325; B 224; W 221; M 319; Du 221. — Signed : *Rembrandt f.* Dated 1636.
Two states; 2d state shown.   *Sewall Coll.*

M. reads the date 1650, but on the impression shown it is evidently 1636.

146. **Landscape with a Milkman.** — Bl 316; B 213; W 210; M 320; Du 210. — Assigned to 1636 by V., to 1650 by M.
Two states; 2d state shown.   *Gray Coll.*

147. **The House on the Banks of the Canal.** — Bl 342 ; B 245 ; W 241 ; Du 242. — Assigned to 1636 by V., rejected by M.
Two states; 1st state shown in photogr. *From Bl.'s R.*

148. **Mennaseh-Ben-Israel.** — Bl 183 ; B 269 ; W 271 ; M 127 ; Du 266. — Signed : *Rembrandt f.* Dated 1636.
Two states; 2d state shown. *Sewall Coll.*

149. **Rembrandt and his Wife.** — Bl 203 ; B 19; W 19 ; M 128 ; Du 19. — Signed : *Rembrandt f.* Dated 1636.
One state only. *Sewall Coll.*

150. **Saskia,** and five other heads. — Bl 249 ; B 365; W 359 ; M 129 ; Du 353. — Signed: *Rembrandt. f.* Dated 1636.
Two states ; 1st state shown. *Sewall Coll.*

151. **Saskia,** and two other heads. — Bl 250 ; B 367 ; W 361 ; M 115 ; Du 355. — Assigned to between 1634 and 1636, probably the latter year, by V., to 1635 by M.
Two states ; 2d state shown. *Sewall Coll.*

152. **Abraham Sending away Hagar and Ishmael.** — Bl 3 ; B 30 ; W 37 ; M 204 ; Du 37. — Signed : *Rembrandt f.* Dated 1637.
One state only. *Sewall Coll.*

153. **A Young Man,** seated, reflecting. — Bl 258 ; B 268 ; W 270 ; M 132 ; Du 282. — Signed : *Rembrandt f.* Dated 1637.
One state only. *Sewall Coll.*

R.'s signature about this time, beginning with plate No. 148, shows curious changes. There is something fanciful in the signatures on plates 149, 150, and 153, which at first sight seems to throw a doubt upon their genuineness.

154. An Old Man, wearing a rich velvet cap. — Bl 269 ; B 313 ; W 314 ; M 131 ; Du 309. — Signed : *Rembrandt f.* Dated 1637.
One state only. *Sewall Coll.*

The name and date have been erased on the impression shown.

155. Saskia, and two other heads of women, one asleep. — Bl 251 ; B 368 ; W 362 ; M 130 ; Du 356. — Signed : *Rembrandt f.* Dated 1637.
One state only. *Sewall Coll.*

156. Adam and Eve. — Bl 1 ; B 28 ; W 35 ; M 206 ; Du 35. — Signed : *Rembrandt. ft.* Dated 1638.
Two states ; 2d state shown : —
(*a.*) Original impression. *Sewall Coll.*
(*b.*) The "deceptive copy," described by Bartsch. *Sewall Coll.*

The copy is shown to put collectors on their guard. Bl., in his "Oeuvre de R." of 1873, reproduces this copy as the original. In the later "Oeuvre" of 1880, the original is reproduced, and the copy is alluded to in the text, but the reader's attention is not called to the error in the previous edition, — a precaution which certainly ought to have been taken, as collectors are likely to be misled, and have been misled, by Bl.'s curious mistake.

157. Abraham caressing Isaac. — Bl 4 ; B 33 ; W 135* ; M 203 ; Du 38. — Signed : *Rembrandt. f.* Assigned to about 1637 to 1639 by V., to 1636 by M.
One state only. *Gray Coll.*

M. is inclined to doubt this piece, and to attribute it to Bol.

158. Joseph telling his Dreams. — Bl 9 ; B 37 ; W 41 ; M 205 ; Du 41. — Signed : *Rembrant f.* Dated 1638.
Two states ; both shown : —
(*a.*) 1st state. *Sewall Coll.*
(*b.*) 2d state. *Sewall Coll.*

The signature is very difficult to make out, and seems to lack the *d,*

159. St. Catherine. (The Little Jewish Bride.) — Bl 200; B 342; W 338; M 135; Du 331. — Signed : *Rembrandt f.* Dated 1638. The whole reversed.
One state only. *Gray Coll.*

The fact that the writing is reversed, but more especially the style of the figures, throws a strong doubt upon the genuineness of the signature.

160. Rembrandt, wearing a mezetin cap with a feather. — Bl 233; B 20; W 20; M 134; Du 20. — Signed : *Rembrandt. f.* Dated 1638.
One state only. *Sewall Coll.*

Bl. describes two states, but according to M. the variations are due to wearing. Upon the impression shown there are some slight retouches in India ink. Most writers go out of their way to give special praise to this awkward and ugly portrait, which cannot possibly represent R. Note the wooden stump of a hand, the unintelligent way in which the folds of the cloak are indicated, and the clumsiness with which the ornaments on the cloak are etched. No beauty of impression can remedy these defects.

161. Rembrandt in a flat cap. — Bl 216; B 26; W 26; M 133; Du 26. — Assigned to 1638 by V. and by M. Signed: *Rembrandt* very faintly in the 1st state; name re-etched by another hand in the 2d state.
Two states; 1st state shown. *Sewall Coll.*

On the impression exhibited the name is not visible. V. considers this piece doubtful.

162. The Sleeping Dog. — Bl 352; B 158; W 155; M 267; Du 154. — Assigned to 1638 by V., to 1640 by M.
Three states; 3d state shown. *Sewall Coll.*

163. The Presentation in the Vaulted Temple. — Bl 22; B 49; W 54; M 208; Du 54. — V. says that the plate is dated 1639, which is a mistake; M. assigns it to 1639.
Four states; three shown.

(*a.*)	1st state, shown in photogr.	*From Bl.'s R.*
(*b.*)	2d state.	*Sewall Coll.*
(*c.*)	3d state,	*Sewall Coll.*

Impression *b* is cut and repaired along the upper margin. Although the plate itself is not dated, there is a reversed copy of it (not described in any catalogue, but an impression in the Museum) which is marked *Rembrand* (no *t*) *f*, 1639.

164. The Death of the Virgin. — Bl 70; B 99; W 104; M 207; Du 102. — Signed : *Rembrandt f.* Dated 1639.
Four states ; 3d state shown.
    (*a.*)   Showing plate marks and full lower margin.
                                        Edward W. Hooper.
    (*b.*)   Without these.   *Sewall Coll.*

The impression lent by Mr. Hooper is shown framed on top of the case in the middle of the room. The wrong use made of the word "state" is well illustrated by the so-called "states" of this plate. Speaking of the 3d state, M. says, "We may, no doubt, regard this as the finished plate, the 1st and 2d states being trial proofs." The so-called 3d state is, therefore, in reality the 1st state.

165. Youth Surprised by Death. — Bl 79; B 109; W 113; M 265; Du 110. — Signed : *Rembrandt f.* Dated 1639.
One state only.   *Sewall Coll.*

166. The Receiver Uytenbogaert. (The Gold-weigher.) — Bl 189; B 281; W 283; M 138; Du 271. — Signed : *Rembrandt ft.* Dated 1639.
Three states ; two shown : —
    (*a.*)   2d state.   *Sewall Coll.*
    (*b.*)   3d state.   *Sewall Coll.*

Concerning Mr. Haden's theories about this plate, viz., that only the head and shoulders of Uytenbogaert are by R., the rest by Bol, see his "Monograph," p. 30.

167. Rembrandt leaning on a stone sill. — Bl 234; B 21; W 21; M 137; Du 21. — Signed : *Rembrandt f.* Dated 1639.
Two states ; 2d state shown.   *Gray Coll.*

168. A Jew with a High Cap. — Bl 101; B 133; W 135; M 140; Du 132. — Signed: *Rembrandt f.* Dated 1639.
One state only.   *Sewall Coll.*

169. A Physician Feeling the Pulse of a Patient.
— Bl 116 ; B 155 ; W 152 ; M 143 ; Du 151. — Assigned
to 1639 by V. and by M.
One state only. Shown in photogravure. *From Bl.'s R.*

Compare with the physician in No. 164.

170. The Decapitation of St. John, the Baptist.
— Bl 40 ; B 92 ; W 97 ; M 209 ; Du 74. — Signed : *Rembrandt f.* Dated **1640.**
Two states ; 2d state shown.   *Sewall Coll.*

M. describes the executioner as "bared to the waist," which is a
mistake. In the 1st state (reproduced in Dutuit's book), the executioner is clothed, as in the state here shown.

171. The Triumph of Mordecai. — Bl 12 ; B 40 ;
W 44 ; M 228 ; Du 48. — Assigned to about 1640 to 1645
by V., to 1651 by M.
One state only.   *Gray Coll.*

According to Bl., there is a 2d state, retouched. The name, Rembrant (without *d*), on the impression shown, has evidently been written
upon it. As portraits of the artist and his wife are so eagerly sought out
in R.'s etchings, it is a wonder that no one has yet pointed out the
resemblance to them which may be detected in the two figures on the
balcony to the right, supposed to represent King Ahasuerus and his
queen Esther.

172. The Virgin Mourning the Death of Jesus.
— Bl 59 ; B 85 ; W 90 ; M 202 ; Du 91. — Assigned to
1640 by V., to 1636 by M.
One state only. Shown in photogravure. *From Bl.'s R.*

Bl. and W. describe two states. Bl., although he retains this plate,
is inclined to attribute it to Bol, and sees Italian influences in it.

173. The Holy Family. (The Virgin with the
Basket of Linen.) — Bl 33 ; B 62 ; W 66 ; M 182 ; Du
65. — Monogram *RHL.* Assigned to 1640 by V., to 1632
by M.
One state only.   *Sewall Coll.*

The monogram favors the earlier year. W. and Bl. describe two states, and M.'s reasons for discarding them hardly seem satisfactory. V. says, " This piece is in the Italian manner."

174. The Crucifixion. Small oval plate. — Bl 54; B 79; W 85; M 222; Du 86. — Assigned to about 1640 by V., to 1648 by M.
Two states ; 2d state shown.   *Sewall Coll.*

175. The Sick Woman. (Saskia Dying.) — Bl 202; B 359; W 353; M 150; Du 347. — Assigned to about 1640 by V., to 1672 by M.
One state only.   *Sewall Coll.*

V. does not share the opinion of Bl. and others, that this is a portrait of Saskia.

176. The Skater. — Bl 121; B 156; W 153; M 103; Du 152. — Assigned to between 1636 and 1640 by V., to 1633 by M.
One state only. Shown in photogravure. *From Bl.'s R.*

177. A Young Woman with a basket. — Bl 240; B 356; W 350; M 151; Du 344. — Assigned to about 1640 by V., to 1642 by M.
Two states; 1st state shown.   *Sewall Coll.*

178. An Old Man with a divided fur cap. — Bl 271; B 265; W 267; M 145; Du 280. — Signed: *Rembrandt f.* Dated **1640.**
One state only.   *Sewall Coll.*

179. The Bull. — Bl 346; B 253; W 249; M 289; Du 250. — Signed: *Rembrandt. f.* 164. (last figure wanting). Date read 1640 by V.; assigned to 1649 by M.
One state only. Shown in photogravure. *From Bl.'s R.*

180. The Canal. — Bl 322; B 221; W 218; M 327; Du 218. — Assigned to about 1640 by V., to 1652 by M.
One state only.   *Sewall Coll.*

181. The Adoration of the Shepherds. Night effect. — Bl 19 ; B 46; W 51 ; M 230 ; Du 51. — Assigned to between 1632 and 1640 by V., to 1652 by M.

Six states ; two shown : —

(*a.*) 2d state (?).	*Sewall Coll.*
(*b.*) 6th state (?).	*Sewall Coll.*

Both M. and Bl. describe six states, but their descriptions are at variance with one another, and do not agree with the prints themselves. The trouble probably arises from the description of trial proofs as states, and from variations in printing. Very likely, impression *a* is the 1st state, and earlier impressions are only trial proofs.

182. The Flight into Egypt. — Bl 27 ; B 54; W 59 ; M 181 ; Du 59. — Assigned to between 1632 and 1640 by V., to 1630 by M.

Six states ; two shown : —

(*a.*) 1st state shown in photogr.	*From Bl.'s R.*
(*b.*) 5th state.	*Sewall Coll.*

183. The Repose in Egypt. Night effect. — Bl 30 ; B 57 ; W 62 ; M 221 ; Du 62. — Assigned to between 1632 and 1640 by V., to 1647 by M.

Three states ; 3d state shown.   *Sewall Coll.*

184. Sketches, including those of two sick women in bed. — Bl 122; B 369 ; W 363 ; M 144 ; Du 357. — Assigned to between 1635 and 1640 by V., to 1639 by M.

One state only : —

(*a.*) Original impression.	*Sewall Coll.*
(*b.*) Photogravure reproduction.	*From Bl.'s R.*

The original and fac-simile are both shown to enable visitors to see all the sketches in an upright position.

185. A Beggar, front view, standing and leaning upon a stick. — Bl 125; B 162 ; W 159; M 33 ; Du 158. — Assigned to between 1635 and 1640 by V., to 1630 by M.

Two states ; 2d state shown.   *Sewall Coll.*

186. A Beggar, in profile, standing and leaning on a stick. — Bl 126; B 163; W 160; M 141; Du 159. — Assigned to between 1632 and 1640 by V., to 1639 by M.
One state only.   *Sewall Coll.*

187. A Beggar, with his wife and child. — Bl 127; B 161; W 158; M 142; Du 157. — Assigned to between 1632 and 1640 by V., to 1639 by M.
One state only. Shown in photogravure. *From Bl.'s R.*

188. A Ragged Peasant, with his hands behind him. — Bl 137; B 172; W 169; M 121; Du 168. — Assigned to between 1632 and 1640 by V., to 1635 by M.
Three states; 3d state shown : —
   (a.) Original impression.   *Sewall Coll.*
   (b.) Photogravure reproduction.   *From Bl.'s R.*

The two impressions have been hung to show the curious difference in the lines to the right of the figure, which may possibly be due to intentional suppression in the printing. A comparison of these impressions with Fig. 6, on Plate I, of M.'s catalogue, will show the unwarrantable carelessness with which many of the figures in this book have been drawn, making them a stumbling-block rather than a help to the collector.

189. A Beggar, with a wooden leg. — Bl 142; B 179; W 176; M 35; Du 175. — Assigned to between 1632 and 1640 by V., to 1630 by M.
Two states; 2d state shown.   *Sewall Coll.*

190. An Old Man lifting his hand to his cap. — Bl 268; B 259; W 260; M 139; W 275. — Assigned to between 1632 and 1640 by V., to 1639 by M.
Two states : —
   (a.) 1st state.   *Sewall Coll.*
   (b.) 2d state.   *Sewall Coll.*

M. allows one state only. Impression *a* is from the plate as left by R.; *b* is from the same plate as finished by G. F. Schmidt towards the end of last century.

191. An Orchard with a Barn. — Bl 330; B 230; W 227; M 316; Du 227. — Assigned to between 1632 and 1640 by V., to 1648 by M.
Two states; 1st state shown in photogr. *From Bl.'s R.*

192. Landscape with a cow drinking. — Bl 337; B 237; W 234; M 318; Du 234. — Assigned to between 1632 and 1640 by V., to 1649 by M.
Four states (?); 3d state shown. *Sewall Coll.*

The cataloguers disagree sadly in their descriptions of the states of this plate. M. allows only two. In the 1st the ground in the lower right corner is only partially shaded, in the 2d there is more shading, but still the extreme lower right corner is blank. M. admits that there are other variations, but he says, "The latest impressions are so bad that I think it is not worth our while to describe them." Nevertheless, both Bl. and Du. reproduce the state of the plate shown in this exhibition, which is certainly later than M.'s 2d state, and there is a still later state which is not quite so bad as to make it unworthy of being looked at. There would seem to be, therefore, at least four states, viz., 1st and 2d as described by M. (for distinctive marks, see his Plate XI, Fig. 57); 3d as here shown; 4th in which the gable end of the building has been worked over, new dry-point work is observable in the trees, and attempts have been made to strengthen the rocks to the left.

193. The Coach Landscape. — B 215; W 212; Du 212. — Assigned to between 1632 and 1640 by V.; rejected by M. and Bl.
One state (?). *Not procurable.*

A photogravure reproduction is given by Dutuit, who, however, also considers the piece doubtful.

194. An Old Man in a high cap, asleep. — Bl 286; B 290; W 292; M 126; Du 287. — Signed: *Rembrandt.* Assigned to between 1632 and 1640 by V., to 1635 by M.
One state only. *Sewall Coll.*

"Somewhat doubtful," according to M.

195. Landscape, with an obelisk. — Bl 328; B 227; W 224; M 324; Du 224. — Assigned to between 1632 and 1640 by V., to 1650 by M.
Two states; 2d state shown. *Sewall Coll.*

196. Jacob and Laban. (Three Oriental Figures.)
— Bl 7 ; B 118 ; W 122 ; M 212 ; Du 119. — Signed, re-
versed : *Rembrandt. f.* Dated **1641.**
Two states; 2d state shown.   *Sewall Coll.*

**197. The Angel Ascending from Tobit and his
Family.** — Bl 16; B 43 ; W 48; M 213 ; Du 46. — Signed :
Rembrandt f. Dated **1641.**
Two states; both shown : —
    (*a.*) 1st state.   *Sewall Coll.*
    (*b.*) 2d state.   *Sewall Coll.*

198. The Virgin and Child on Clouds. — Bl 32 ;
B 61 ; W 65 ; M 211 ; Du 64.
One state only.   *Gray Coll.*

199. The Baptism of the Eunuch. — Bl 69 ; B 98 ;
W 103 ; M 210 ; Du 101. — Signed : *Rembrandt. f.* Dated
1641.
Two states ; 2d state shown.   *Sewall Coll.*

200. The Schoolmaster. (The Hurdy-Gurdy Player.)
— Bl 99 ; B 128 ; W 131 ; M 271 ; Du 128. — Signed :
Rembrandt f. Dated **1641.**
One state only.   *Sewall Coll.*

201. The Star of the Kings. — Bl 85 ; B 113 ; W
117 ; M 293 ; Du 114. — Assigned to 1641 by V., to 1652
by M.
One state only.   *Sewall Coll.*

202. The Large Lion Hunt. — Bl 86 ; B 114 ; W
118 ; M 272 ; Du 115. — Signed : *Rembrandt f.* Dated
1641.
One state only.   *Sewall Coll.*

203. The Small Lion Hunt, with a lioness. — Bl
87 ; B 115 ; W 119 ; M 273 ; Du 116. — Assigned to 1641
by V. and by M.
Two states; 2d state shown.   *Sewall Coll.*

204. **Another Lion Hunt.** Companion to No. 203.
— Bl 88 ; B 116 ; W 120 ; M 274 ; Du 117. — Assigned to
1641 by V. and by M.
One state only. *Sewall Coll.*

The three " Lion Hunts," Nos. 202, 203, and 204, as well as No.
205, are generally described as " in the manner of Rubens."

205. **Battlepiece.** — Bl 89 ; B 117 ; W 121 ; M 275 ;
Du 118. — Assigned to 1641 by V. and by M.
Three states ; 2d state shown. *Sewall Coll.*

206. **Cornelis Claesz. Anslo.** — Bl 170 ; B 271 ; W
273 ; M 146 ; Du 254. — Signed : *Rembrandt f.* Dated
1641.
Four states ; two shown : —
  (*a.*) 3d state. *Sewall Coll.*
  (*b.*) 4th state. *Sewall Coll.*

207. **Portrait of a Boy.** — Bl 177 ; B 310 ; W 311 ;
M 148 ; Du 306. — Signed : *Rembrandt. f.* Dated 1641.
One state only. *Sewall Coll.*

Called also, erroneously, according to V., " Portrait of William II."

208. **A Man with Crucifix and Chain.** (The Writer.)
— Bl 257 ; B 261 ; W 263 ; M 147 ; Du 277. — Signed :
Rembrandt f. Dated 1641.
Four states ; 2d state shown. *Sewall Coll.*

209. **A Man Playing Cards.** — Bl 104 ; B 136 ; W
137 ; M 269 ; Du 135. — Signed : *Rembrandt f.* Dated
1641.
Three states : —
  (*a.*) 1st state. *Sewall Coll.*
  (*b.*) 2d state. *Sewall Coll.*
  (*c.*) 3d state. *Sewall Coll.*

Impression *b* is partly washed with India ink.

210. **View of Amsterdam.** — Bl 313; B 210; W 207 ; M 304 ; Du 207.— Assigned to 1641 by V., to 1640 by M.
One state only.   *Sewall Coll.*

About one quarter of an inch has been cut off on the left side of the impression shown.

211. **Landscape** with a cottage and a hay-barn. — Bl 327 ; B 225 ; W 222 ; M 306; Du 222. — Signed : *Rembrandt f.* Dated 1641.
One state only.   *Gray Coll.*

212. **Landscape** with a mill sail. — Bl 326 ; B 226 ; W 223; M 307; Du 223. — Signed : *Rembrandt f.* Dated 1641.
One state only.   *Sewall Coll.*

213. **The Mill.** (Rembrandt's Mill.) — Bl 333 ; B 233; W 230; M 305; Du 230.— Signed : *Rembrandt f.* Dated 1641.
One state only.   *Sewall Coll.*

214. **The Resurrection of Lazarus.** (Small plate.) — Bl 47; B 72; W 76; M 215; Du 78. — Signed : *Rembrandt f.* Dated 1642.
One state only.   *Sewall Coll.*

There exists a reversed copy not described by M.

215. **The Descent from the Cross.** A sketch. — Bl 57; B 82; W 87; M 216; Du 89. — Signed : *Rembrandt f.* Dated 1642.
One state only.   *Sewall Coll.*

216. **St. Jerome,** writing near a large tree. — Bl 74 ; B 103; W 108; M 223; Du 106. — Signed in 2d state : *Rembrandt f.* Dated 1642 (?) or 1648 (?).
Two states ; 2d state shown.   *Sewall Coll.*

V. specially says that the date is 1642, and not 1648. M. neverthe-less reads the latter date, and, on the evidence of the impression shown, he is certainly right. He thinks, however, that the etched work in this plate is earlier than the dry pointing (which includes the date), and bears a resemblance to the work of 1642.

217. St. Jerome, in meditation. — Bl 76; B 105; W 110; M 214; Du 108. — Signed: *Rembrandt f.* Dated **1642.**
Two states; 2d state shown. *Sewall Coll.*

218. The Spanish Gipsy. — Bl 83; B 120; W 124; M 285; Du 121. — Assigned to 1642 by V., to 1647 by M.
One state only. Shown in photogravure. *From Bl.'s R.*

219. The Flute Player. — Bl 153; B 188; W 185; M 268; Du 185. — Signed in 2d state: *Rembrandt f.* Dated **1642.**
Four states; two shown: —
    (*a.*) 1st state. Shown in photogr. *From Bl.'s R.*
    (*b.*) 4th state. *Sewall Coll.*

M. reads 1640, but the date is clearly 1642, with the 2 reversed.

220. The Monk in the Cornfield. — Bl 152; B 187; W 184; M 282; Du 184. — Assigned to 1642 by V., to 1646 by M.
One state only. *Not shown.*

221. The Shepherds in the Wood. (The Old Man Asleep.) — Bl 154; B 189; W 186; M 281; Du 186. — Assigned to 1642 by V., to 1646 by M.
One state only. *Not shown.*

222. A Man in an Arbor. — Bl 262; B 257; W 258; M 152; Du 273. — Signed: *Rembrandt f.* Dated 1642.
One state only. *Gray Coll.*

223. **Sketches** of a tree, etc. — Bl 349 ; B 372 ; W 366 ; M 154 ; Du 360. — Assigned to 1643 by V. for the whole, by M. for the tree.
One state only.   *Sewall Coll.*

224. **The Hog.** — Bl 350 ; B 157 ; W 154 ; M 277 ; Du 153. — Signed : *Rembrandt f.* Dated **1643**.
Two states ; 1st state shown.   *Sewall Coll.*

225. **The Three Trees.** — Bl 315 ; B 212 ; W 209 ; M 309 ; Du 209. — Signed : *Rembrandt.* Dated **1643**.
One state only.
   (*a.*) Impression from plate.   *Sewall Coll.*
   (*b.*) Counterproof.   *Sewall Coll.*

226. **The Shepherd and his Family.** — Bl 321 ; B 220 ; W 217 ; M 310 ; Du 217. — Signed : *Rembrandt f.* Dated **1644**.
One state only.   *Sewall Coll.*

227. **Abraham Speaking to Isaac.** — Bl 5 ; B 34 ; W 38 ; M 220 ; Du 39. — Signed : *Rembrant* (no *d*). Dated **1645**.
One state only.   *Sewall Coll.*

228. **The Repose in Egypt.** — Bl 31 ; B 58 ; W 63 ; M 218 ; Du 63. — *Rembrandt. f.* Dated **1645**.
One state only.   *Sewall Coll.*

229. **St. Peter.** — Bl 67 ; B 96 ; W 101 ; M 219 ; Du 99. — Signed : *Rembrandt f.* **1645**.
One state only.   *Sewall Coll.*

V. is particular to state that the date on this plate is 1655, and not 1645. On the impression shown, however, as well as on the reproductions given by Bl. and Du., the date is very clearly 1645.

230. **An Old** Man, meditating. — Bl 111 ; B 147 ; W 145 ; M 156 ; Du 143. — Assigned to 1645 by V., to 1646 by M.
Two states ; 2d state shown in photogr. *From Bl.'s R.*

231. **Jan Cornelis Sylvius.** — Bl 187; B 280; W 282; M 155; Du 269. — Signed: *Rembrandt.* Dated 1646.
Two states; 2d state shown. *Sewall Coll.*

232. **Rembrandt, drawing on a plate.** — Bl 228; W 32; M 173; Du 32. —Signed: *Rembrandt f.* Dated 1645 (or 1658?).
One state only. Shown in photogravure. *From Bl.'s R.*

The reproduction shown is not from the original, of which only one or two copies are known, but from a copy by Basan. On this copy the date is plainly 1645. M. and Du. claim, however, that the original is dated 1658. "Doubtful," says V., "I do not believe it is by R." How this hideous and ill-drawn portrait came to be admitted among R.'s work at all, it would be difficult to say. Still, all the catalogues, except B., admit it, although they cannot even agree upon the meaning of the head covering worn by the man, one (W.) declaring it to be "a cap, the end of which comes down on the right"; a second (Bl.) "un bonnet de coton, dont la mèche penche sur le côté droit" (say a cotton nightcap); a third (M.) "a soft cap with a feather passing across the front," while the fourth (Du.), more guarded than his brethren, contents himself by describing it as "une espèce de bonnet." If Basan has copied the signature with only approximate correctness, that alone ought to condemn the plate.

233. **Six's Bridge.** — Bl 311; B 208; W 205; M 313; Du 205. — Signed: *Rembrandt f.* Dated 1645.
Three states; 3d state shown. *Sewall Coll.*

234. **View of Omval.** — Bl 312; B 209; W 206; M 311; Du 206. — Signed: *Rembrant* (no *d*). Dated 1645.
One state only.
(*a.*) Impression from the plate in its original condition. *Sewall Coll.*
(*b.*) Impression from the disfigured plate. *Sewall Coll.*

Impression *b* is the one described by M. from the collection of the Rev. Burleigh James. Mr. Haden says that "Omval is not a village, but a bend in the river Amstel, near Amsterdam," and that, therefore, the plate ought to be called "The Omval." V., on the contrary, himself a Hollander, speaks of the subject quite explicitly as "the view of Omval, a village in the environs of Amsterdam."

235. **Landscape**, with a man sketching. — Bl 320 ; B 219 ; W 216 ; M 315 ; Du 216. — Assigned to 1645 by V., to 1646 by M.
One state only.   *Sewall Coll.*

236. **The Cottages near the Canal.** (The Sail Boat.) — Bl 329 ; B 228 ; W 225 ; M 314 ; Du 225. — Assigned to 1645 by V. and by M.
Two states ; 1st state shown.   *Sewall Coll.*

V. thinks this may be a view of Hillegom, the home of the Six family.

237. **The Boat under the Trees.** (A Grotto with a Brook. The Boathouse.) — Bl 331 ; B 231 ; W 228 ; M 312 ; Du 228. — Signed : *Rembrandt.* Dated **1645.**
One state only. (Late impression shown.) *Sewall Coll.*

238. **Study** of a youth seated. (Study for the Prodigal Son.) — Bl 158 ; B 193 ; W 190 ; M 279 ; Du 190. — Signed : *Rembrandt. f.* Dated **1646.**
One state only.   *Sewall Coll.*

239. **Study** of a youth seated on the ground. — Bl 160 ; B 196 ; W 193 ; M 278 ; Du 193. — Signed : *Rembrandt. f.* Dated **1646.**
One state only.   *Sewall Coll.*

240. **Studies** of two boys ; a go-cart, etc., in the background. — Bl 159 ; B 194 ; W 191 ; M 280 ; Du 191. — Assigned to 1646 by V. and by M.
Two states ; 2d state shown.   *Sewall Coll.*

M. claims that in the background we have a sketch " executed at a much earlier time, and which was entirely overlooked when R. worked these studies upon the plate," all of which is contradicted by the composition of the plate and the way in which the cavity of the fireplace, instead of being " entirely overlooked," is made to serve a purpose in throwing the standing figure into relief.

241. **A Beggar Woman.** — Bl 134 ; B 170 ; W 167 ; M 157 ; Du 166. — Signed: *Rembrandt. f.* Dated **1646**. One state only. *Sewall Coll.*

242. **De Ledekant.** — Bl 151 ; B 186 ; W 183 ; M 283 ; Du 183. — Signed : *Rembrandt f.* Dated **1646**. Three states. *Not shown.*

243. **Portrait of Jan Six.** — Bl 184 ; B 285 ; W 287 ; M 159 ; Du 267. — Signed : *Rembrandt. f.* Dated **1647**. Three states ; two shown : —
   (*a.*) 2d state. *Gray Coll.*
   (*b.*) 3d state. *Sewall Coll.*

244. **Portrait of Dr. Ephraim Bonus.** (The Jew at the Baluster.) — Bl 172 ; B 278 ; W 280 ; M 158 ; Du 256. Signed : *Rembrandt. f.* Dated **1647**. Two states ; 2d state shown. *Gray Coll.*

245. **Portrait of Jan Asselyn.** — Bl 171 ; B 277 ; W 279 ; M 161 ; Du 255. — Signature and date incomplete. Assigned to 1647 by V., to 1648 by M. Three states ; two shown : —
   (*a.*) 1st state in photogravure. *From Bl.'s R.*
   (*b.*) 3d state. *Gray Coll.*

Bl. describes four and speaks of a 5th state.

246. **Portrait of Dr. Jan Antonides Van der Linden.** — Bl 181 ; B 264 ; W 266 ; M 167 ; Du 264. — Assigned to between 1647 and 1656 by V., to 1653 by M. Six states ; state shown? *Sewall Coll.*

It is difficult to make out the states of this plate from the descriptions. The impression shown would appear to be between M.'s 3d and 4th states.

247. **The Synagogue.** — Bl 98 ; B 126 ; W 130 ; M 288 ; Du 127. — Signed : *Rembrandt. f.* Dated **1648**. Three states ; 2d (?) state shown. *Sewall Coll.*

248. Medea. (The Marriage of Jason and Crëusa.) — Bl 82; B 112; W 116; M 286; Du 113. — Signed and dated in 4th state: *Rembrandt. f.* **1648.**
Five states; four shown : —

(*a.*)	1st state.	*Gray Coll.*
(*b.*)	3d state.	*Sewall Coll.*
(*c.*)	4th state.	*Sewall Coll.*
(*d.*)	5th state.	*Sewall Coll.*

M. describes Medea, who is seen advancing in the lower right corner, as " holding a handkerchief to her face, as if weeping." The impressions shown demonstrate that this description is not correct.

249. The Phœnix. (The Allegorical Tomb.) — Bl 80; B 110; W 114; M 296; Du 111 — Signed : *Rembrand f.* (apparently no *t*). Date read 1648 by V., 1658 by M , still differently by others.
One state only. Shown in photogravure. *From Bl.'s R.*

250. Beggars at the Door of a House. — Bl 146; B 176; W 173; M 287; Du 172. — Signed : *Rembrandt. f.* Dated **1648.**
Two states ; 2d state shown : —

(*a.*)	Printed in black.	*Sewall Coll.*
(*b.*)	Printed in red.	*Gray Coll.*

251. Doctor Faustus. — Bl 84 ; B 270; W 272; M 291; Du 259. — Assigned to between 1647 and 1650 by V., to 1651 by M.
Three states : —

(*a.*)	1st state.	*Sewall Coll.*
(*b.*)	2d state.	*Sewall Coll.*
(*c.*)	3d state.	*Gray Coll.*

252. An Artist (R.?) Drawing from a Model. — Bl 157 ; B 192; W 189; M 284; Du 189. — Assigned to between 1646 and 1648 by V., to 1647 by M.
Two states ; 2d state shown.   *Sewall Coll.*

M. thinks that the work on the 1st state of this abandoned plate is by R., and that possibly the additional work in the 2d state is by an assistant. Mr. Haden opines ("Monograph," p. 31) that R. only laid in the subject, as shown in the unfinished part, and that Bol was charged with finishing it. In accordance with his theory, that R. ceased to avail himself of pupil work in his etchings about 1639, he assigns this plate to an earlier period than either V. or M.

253. Rembrandt, drawing at a window. — Bl 235; B 22; W 22; M 160; Du 22. — Signed: *Rembrandt f.* Dated **1648.**

Seven states; two shown: —
(*a.*) 2d state.   Shown in photogr.   *From Bl.'s R.*
(*b.*) 6th state.   *Sewall Coll.*

M.'s description of the states of this plate is most unsatisfactory. Bl. describes ten states, of which the examples shown seem to be respectively the 6th and 9th. M. thinks that the variations after his 3d state are not by R.

254. Two Beggars, a man and a woman. — Bl 145; B 183; W 180; M 13; Du 179. — Assigned to about 1648 by V.; to 1629 by M.

One state only.   Shown in photogravure.   *From Bl.'s R.*

255. Sketches of Two Beggars. — Bl 147; B 182; W 179; M 11; Du 178. — Assigned to about 1648 by V., to 1629 by M.

One state only.   Shown in photogravure.   *From Bl.'s R.*

256. A Sick Beggar and his Wife. — Bl 148; B 185; W 182; Du 181. — Assigned to about 1648 by V., rejected by M.

One state only.   Shown in photogravure.   *From Bl.'s R.*

257. The Fat Beggar. — Bl 149; B 184; W 181; M 9; Du 180. — Assigned to about 1648 by V., to 1629 by M.

One state only.   Shown in photogravure.   *From Bl.'s R.*

258. A Beggar, in a cloak, standing, a woman in the distance. — Bl 150 ; M 8 ; Du 182. — Assigned to about 1648 by V., to 1629 by M.
One state only. Shown in photogravure. *From Bl.'s R.*

259. St. Jerome, reading. — Bl 75 ; B 104 ; W 109 ; M 234 ; Du 107. — Assigned to 1650 by V., to 1653 by M.
Two states ; 2d state shown : —
> (*a.*) Early impression on dark paper. *Sewall Coll.*
> (*b.*) Somewhat later impression washed here and and there with India ink. *Gray Coll.*

This piece is usually said to be "in the manner of Dürer." Mr. Haden affirms that it is from a drawing by Titian, " differing in nothing from the etching except in the absence of the lion, and the presence of a recumbent figure of Venus in place of the saint." V. has it that " the landscape is quite in the style of the view of Ransdorp, Bl. 319 [No. 264 of this catalogue], of which we here see also the tower."

260. Jesus Appearing to His Disciples. — Bl 64 ; B 89 ; W 94 ; M 225 ; Du 96. — Signed *Rembrandt. f.* Dated **1650.**
One state only. *Sewall Coll.*

261. The Shell. — Bl 353 ; B 159 ; W 156 ; M 290 ; Du 155. — Signed : *Rembrandt. f.* Dated **1650.**
Two states ; 2d state shown. *Sewall Coll.*

262. A Young Man, with a game pouch. — Bl 253 ; B 258 ; W 259 ; Du 274. — Dated **1650.**
One state only. Shown in photogr. *From Bl.'s R.*

Rejected by M., and generally doubted by the other cataloguers. The date upon the plate certainly is not by R.

263. The Three Cottages. — Bl 318 ; B 217 ; W 214 ; M 325 ; Du 214. — Signed : *Rembrandt f.* Dated **1650.**
Three states ; 2d state. *Gray Coll.*

264. Landscape, with a square tower. — Bl 319 ; B 218 ; W 215 ; M 321 ; Du 215. — Signed : *Rembrandt. f.* Dated **1650**.

Four states ; 4th state shown. *Gray Coll.*

According to V., this is a view in Ransdorp. See No. 259.

265. The Canal with the Swans. — Bl 335 ; B 235 ; W 232 ; M 322 ; Du 232. — Signed : *Rembrandt f.* Dated **1650**.

Two states ; 2d state shown. *Sewall Coll.*

266. Landscape, with a large boat. — Bl 336 ; B 236 ; W 233 ; M 323 ; Du 233. — Signed : *Rembrandt. f.* **1650**. Two states ; 2d state shown. *Sewall Coll.*

Nos. 265 and 266, as the exhibition shows, form in reality the two halves of a little panorama.

267. The Hunter. — Bl 314 ; B 211 ; W 208 ; M 329 ; Du 208. — Assigned to 1650 by V., to 1653 by M.

Two states ; 2d state shown. *Sewall Coll.*

Mr. Haden is of opinion that the motive for the background in this plate, as in several other plates, was appropriated by R. from some design by Titian or Campagnola.

268. Landscape, with a ruined tower. — Bl 324 ; B 223 ; W 220 ; M 317 ; Du 220. — Assigned to 1650 by V., to 1648 by M.

Four states ; 1st state shown. *Sewall Coll.*

According to V., this is a view of the village of Loenen. In later and more frequent states, the tower appears in a ruined condition, hence the name of the piece. The impression shown, it will be observed, has been cut on the right side, and then joined together again, but the pieces seem to be printed on paper of different quality. Curiously enough, the impression from which Bl.'s reproduction was made has evidently been cut and joined together again in precisely the same place.

269.   Christ Healing the Sick.   (The   Hundred
Guilders Piece.) — Bl 49 ; B 74 ; W 78 ; M 224 ; Du 77.
— Assigned to about 1650 by V., to 1649 by M.
  Two states ; 2d state shown : —
  (*a.*)   Impression slightly washed with India ink.
                                                Sewall Coll.
  (*b.*)   Later impression?   *Gray Coll.*
  (*c.*)   Very late impression, from the rusted plate.
                                                Gray Coll.

According to Mr. Haden ("Monograph," p. 35), fine impressions
from this celebrated plate in the 2d state are preferable to those in the
1st state.   There is a remarkable difference in the measurements given
of this plate.   All measurements of prints must necessarily be approximate only, as the stretching of the dampened paper and its shrinkage
upon drying are beyond control or calculation.   Differences of one cen-
timetre, however, seem unexplainable.   The true approximate measurements, based upon the four impressions here shown, are : − .395 at the
bottom; − .397 at the top; − .277 at the right; − .281 at the left.
Only Bartsch and Claussin, and Dutuit, give measurements corresponding
to these, viz., the two former (ignoring the difference between top and
bottom and right and left) 14 p., 8 l. in breadth, 10 p. 5 l. in height;
the latter − .396 by 281.   W. gives 15.20 inches at bottom, 15.30 at
top, 10.90 for height; M. − .385 by − .279; Bl. − .387 by − .281.

269 A.   Christ Healing the Sick, as retouched by
Capt. Wm. Baillie.
  (*a.*)   The whole plate.   *Sewall Coll.*
  (*b.*)   The central group.   Square top.   *Sewall Coll.*
  (*c.*)   Upper left hand group.   *Sewall Coll.*
  (*d.*)   Lower left hand group.   *Sewall Coll.*
  (*e.*)   Right hand group.   *Sewall Coll.*
  (*f.*)   The central group.   Arched top.   *Sewall Coll.*

269 B.   Christ Healing the Sick.   Copies.
  (*a.*)   By Thomas Worlidge.   *Sewall Coll.*
  (*b.*)   By Leopold Flameng.   *Sewall Coll.*
  (*c*)   By photogravure.   *Sewall Coll.*

REMBRANDT'S ETCHINGS,

ARRANGED IN CHRONOLOGICAL ORDER ACCORDING TO
C. VOSMÆR'S LIST, Continued. (Cases 1 to 10.)

270. **An Old Man,** with his hands upon a book. —
Bl 287; B 267; W 269; Du 281. — Assigned to between
1640 and 1650 by V., rejected by M. *Not procurable.*

271. **The Two Houses,** with pointed gables. — Bl
317; B 214; W 211; Du 211. — Assigned to between
1640 and 1650 by V., rejected by M.
One state only. Shown in photogr. *From Bl.'s R.*

Bl. and M. both think that this etching may be by Philip de Koninck.

272. **The House with Three Chimneys.** — Bl
(under 339); B 250; W 246; Du 247. — Assigned to
between 1640 and 1650 by V., rejected by M.
One state only. Shown in photogr. *From Bl.'s R.*

273. **Tobit Blind,** feeling for the door, with a dog
beside him. — Bl 15; B 42; W 46; M 226; Du 45. —
Signed: *Rembrandt f.* Dated **1651.**
Two states; 2d state shown. *Sewall Coll.*

274. **Tobit Blind,** feeling for the door. — Bl 14; B
153; W 47; M 180; Du 149. — Assigned to about 1651
by V., to 1630 by M.
Four states; 2d state shown in photogr. *From Bl.'s R.*

275. The Flight into Egypt. Night effect. — Bl
26 ; B 53 ; W 58 ; M 227 ; Du 58. — Signed : *Rembrandt f.*
Dated 1651.
Four states ; two shown : —
   (*a.*)   1st state in photogravure.   *From Bl.'s R.*
   (*b.*)   4th state.   *Sewall Coll.*

276. Portrait of Clement de Jonghe. — Bl 180 ;
B 272 ; W 274 ; M 164 ; Du 263. — Signed: *Rembrandt. f.*
Dated 1651.
Six states ; three shown : —
   (*a.*)   1st state.   *Sewall Coll.*
   (*b.*)   3d state.   *Sewall Coll.*
   (*c.*)   6th state.   *Sewall Coll.*

M. thinks that the alterations of the 3d and later states were not
made by R.

277. The Goldweigher's Field. — Bl 334 ; B 234 ;
W 231 ; M 326 ; Du 231. — Signed : *Rembrandt.* Dated
1651.
One state only.   *Sewall Coll.*

A view, according to V., of the country seat of the Receiver Uytenbogaert (The Goldweigher), with the city of Naarden in the left distance. Mr. Haden would have it called "The Château," possibly
"Six's Château."

278. David Kneeling in Prayer. — Bl 13 ; B 41 ;
W 45 ; M 232 ; Du 44. — Signed: *Rembrandt. f.* Dated
1652.
Two states ; state shown ?   *Sewall Coll.*

If the insignificant distinctions which separate the "states" of this
plate are to be taken into account, the impression shown will have to
be placed between the 1st and 2d states, for while the small white spot
on the left of the plate has been worked over, the back of David's
night-gown shows no "slipped stroke."

279. Jesus Disputing with the Doctors — Bl 36 ;
B 65 ; W 69 ; M 231 ; Du 68. — Signed : *Rembrandt. f.*
Dated 1652.
Three states ; 2d state shown.   *Sewall Coll.*

280. **Jesus Christ Preaching.** (The Little La
Tombe.) — Bl 39; B 67; W 71; M 229; Du 71. — Assigned to 1652 by V. and by M.
One state only : —
  (*a.*) Impression from the plate with considerable
      bur still on it.   *Sewall Coll.*
  (*b.*) Impression after the bur had all worn off.
                          Sewall Coll.

This plate is sometimes called " Le Petit La Tombe " (The Little La
Tombe), which has been improved into " La Petite Tombe " (The Little
Tombstone, or Tomb). It is said to have been owned in R.'s time by a
dealer in prints, named La Tombe or de la Tombe, and, to distinguish
it, possibly, from other larger plates belonging to him, was called " The
Little La Tombe," which became in French "le petit La Tombe."

281. **Peasant with his Wife and Children.** — Bl
120; B 131; W 134; M 153; Du 131. — Assigned to 1652
by V., to 1643 by M.
One state only.   *Sewall Coll.*

282. **The Vista.** (The Bouquet of Trees.) — Bl 323;
B 222; W 219; M 328; Du 219. — Signed, in 3d state :
Rembrandt f. Dated **1652.**
Three states ; 3d state shown.   *Sewall Coll.*

283. **Landscape,** with an old square tower. — Bl 338;
B 238; W 235; Du 235. — Signed : *Remb. f.* Dated
1653.
One state only. Shown in photogravure. *From Bl.'s R.*

The date is hardly legible. M., who rejects the print, is inclined to
read it 1651.

284. **The Circumcision.** — Bl 20; B 47; W 52; M
239; Du 52. — Signed and dated twice : *Rembrandt. f.*
1654.
Two states ; both shown : —
  (*a.*) 1st state.   *Sewall Coll.*
  (*b.*) 2d state.   *Sewall Coll.*

285. The Nativity. — Bl 18; B 45; W 50; M 238; Du 50. — Signed : *Rembrandt. f.* Assigned to 1654 by V. and by M.

Two states ; both shown : —

    (*a.*) 1st state.   *Sewall Coll.*

    (*b.*) 2d state.   *Sewall Coll.*

286. The Flight into Egypt. (The Holy Family Crossing a Rill.) — Bl 28 ; B 55 ; W 60 ; M 240 ; Du 60. — Signed : *Rembrandt f.* Dated **1654.**

One state only.   *Sewall Coll.*

287. The Flight into Egypt, in the manner of Elsheimer. — Bl 29 ; B 56 ; W 61 ; M 236 ; Du 61. — Assigned by V., for the figures, to about 1652 to 1654, by M. to 1653.

Five states ; 5th state shown (?).   *Sewall Coll.*

It is well known that this plate was originally etched by Hercules Seghers, and only altered and adopted or appropriated by R. The changes in the 4th and later states possibly not by R.

288. The Holy Family with the Cat, or with the serpent. — Bl 34 ; B 63 ; W 67 ; M 241 ; Du 66.

Two states ; 1st state shown.   *Sewall Coll.*

For a list of the plagiarisms charged against R., see Mr. Haden's " Monograph," pp. 18 and 19. In this plate he is said to have imitated Mantegna's " Virgin and Child," B. 8. The reduced copy of this engraving, exhibited below the etching, will enable the visitor to judge for himself of the extent of imitation practised by R. in this case.

289. Jesus Disputing with the Doctors. The smaller plate. — Bl 35 ; B 64 ; W 68 ; M 245 ; Du 67. — Signed : *Rembrandt. f.* Dated **1654.**

One state only.   *Sewall Coll.*

290. Jesus Brought Home from the Temple. (Jesus and his parents returning from Egypt.) — Bl 38 ; B 60 ; W 64 ; M 244 ; Du 70. — Signed : *Rembrandt. f.* Dated **1654.**

One state only.   *Sewall Coll.*

291. **The Descent from the Cross.** Night effect.
— Bl 58; ·B 83; W 88; M 242; Du 90. — Signed: *Rembrandt. f.* Dated 1654.
One state only : —
(*a.*) Early impression, showing considerable bur.
Sewall Coll.
(*b.*) Later impression. *Sewall Coll.*

M. describes the figure spreading a sheet to receive the body as "a woman with a headdress like that of a nun." The impressions here exhibited, and more especially impression *b*, clearly show that it is an elderly man with wrinkled brow and heavy beard.

292. **The Entombment.** — Bl 61; B 86; W 91; M 233; Du 93. — Assigned to 1654 by V., to 1652 by M.
Four states; 3d state shown. *Sewall Coll.*

The impression exhibited has in parts been washed with India ink. The 4th state, M. thinks, is not due to R.

293. **Jesus and the Disciples at Emmaus.** — Bl 63; B 87; W 92; M 237; Du 94. — Signed: *Rembrandt. f.* Dated 1654.
Two states; both shown : —
(*a.*) 1st state in photogravure. *From Bl.'s R.*
(*b.*) 2d state. *Sewall Coll.*

294. **The Kolf Players.** — Bl 97; B 125; W 129; M 294; Du 126. — Signed: *Rembrandt f.* Dated 1654.
Two states; both shown : —
(*a.*) 1st state. *Sewall Coll.*
(*b.*) 2d state. *Sewall Coll.*

295. **Portrait of Titus, R.'s Son.** — Bl 236; B 11; W 11; M 165; Du 11. — Assigned to about 1652 to 1654 by V., to 1652 by M.
One state only. Shown in photogravure.
From Bl.'s R.

296. Four Plates for a Spanish Book (i. e. Menassch-Ben-Israel's " Piedra gloriosa "). — Bl 8 ; B 36 ; W 40; M 247 ; Du 47.— Signed: *Rembrandt. f.* Dated **1655.**

A.   *The Image which Nebuchadnezzar saw.*
Five states ; 5th state shown.   *Sewall Coll.*
  B.   *Ezekiel's Vision.*
Three states; 3d state shown.
  (*a.*)   Impression on paper.   *Sewall Coll.*
  (*b.*)   Impression on vellum.   *Sewall Coll.*
  c.   *Jacob's Ladder.*
Three states ; 2d state shown.   *Sewall Coll.*
  D.   *David and Goliath.*
Three states ; 3d state shown.   *Sewall Coll.*

297. The Agony in the Garden. — Bl 50; B 75 ; W 79 ; M 251 ; Du 82. — Signed : *Rembrandt. f.* Dated 165 . — Assigned to 1655 by V., to 1657 by M.
One state only.   *Sewall Coll.*

The last figure is wanting in the date.

298. Abraham's Sacrifice. — Bl 6 ; B 35 ; W 39 ; M 246 ; Du 40. — Signed : *Rembrandt f.*   Dated **1655.**
One state only.   *Sewall Coll.*

Mr. Haden makes Gerbrand van den Eeckhout the author of this composition.

299. Christ presented to the People. — Bl 51 ; B 76 ; W 80 ; M 248 ; Du 83. — Signed and dated in the 6th state : *Rembrandt f.* **1655.**
Seven states ; three shown : —
  (*a.*)   1st state.   Flameng's copy.   *Sewall Coll.*
  (*b.*)   3d state.   *Sewall Coll.*
  (*c.*)   7th state.   *Sewall Coll.*

M. opines that the variations after the 4th state are not by R., an opinion evidently not shared by Bl. A remote resemblance in the general ordering of the plate to Lucas van Leyden's engraving of the same scene, has caused it to be spoken of as " in the manner of Lucas van Leyden." The small autotype of Lucas's composition, placed alongside of R.'s etching, or rather dry-point, will enable the visitor to form an independent judgment of this charge of plagiarism.

300. The Three Crosses. — Bl 53 ; B 78 ; W 81 ; M 235 ; Du 85. — Signed and dated in the 3d and later states : *Rembrandt. f.* **1655.**

Five states ; two shown : —

    (*a.*) 3d state in photogravure.   *From Bl.'s R.*
    (*b.*) 4th state. With a margin.   *Edw. W. Hooper.*
    (*c.*) 4th state. On brownish paper.   *Sewall Coll.*

Impression *b* is shown framed on a stand on the table. M. and others read the date 1653, but the line which apparently makes a 3 of the second 5 is evidently part of a shading line in the foreground. It is well known that the theories and differences of opinion called forth by this plate are of the most extraordinary kind, and students will not fail, therefore, to read what has been said about it by Hamerton, Blanc, Haden ("Monograph," pp. 37 and 51), and others.

301. The Little Goldsmith. — Bl 94 ; B 123 ; W 127 ; M 295 ; Du 124. — Signed : *Rembrandt f.* Dated **1655.**
One state only. (Two impressions shown.) *Sewall Coll.*

V., overlooking the name and date, which are almost illegible, assigns this plate to 1654.

302. Portrait of Thomas Jacobsz. Haring. (Young Haring.) — Bl 179 ; B 275 ; W 277 ; M 169 ; Du 262. — Signed : *Rembrandt. f.* Dated **1655.**

Five states ; three shown : —

    (*a.*) 1st state, in photogravure.   *From Bl.'s R.*
    (*b.*) 2d state.   *Sewall Coll.*
    (*c.*) 4th state.   *Gray Coll.*

M. doubts whether the 2d state is by R., and ascribes all later states to other hands.

303. Portrait of Jacob Haring. (Old Haring.) — Bl 178 ; B 274 ; W 276 ; M 168 ; Du 261. — Assigned to 1655 by V. and by M.
One state only ?   *Sewall Coll.*

W. and Bl. describe three states. The impression exhibited, which is on vellum (or on pig-skin?), shows certain peculiarities which seem to distinguish it from these states, and place it between the 2d and 3d. Notice especially the absence of the harsh dry-point lines in the face and hair. The frequent occurrence of impressions on vellum about this time is worthy of remark. One of the plates for a Spanish book is printed on it (1655), and it was used for some of the earlier states of the Three Crosses. See also next number.

304. Portrait of Abraham Francen. — (Frans, Fransz). — Bl 176 ; B 273 ; W 275 ; M 172 ; Du 260. — Assigned to probably 1655, certainly not before 1654, by V., to 1656 by M.

Ten states ; three shown : —
 (*a*.) 4th state. On vellum (or pig-skin ?). *Gray Coll.*
 (*b*.) 8th state. *Sewall Coll.*
 (*c*.) 10th state. *Sewall Coll.*

M. thinks that after the 4th state, the plate was worked upon by other hands.

305. Abraham Entertaining the Angels. — Bl 2 ; B 29 ; W 36 ; M 250 ; Du 36. — Signed : *Rembrandt. f.* Dated **1656.**
One state only. *Sewall Coll.*

306. Portrait of John Lutma, the Elder. — Bl 182 ; B 276; W 278 ; M 171 ; Du 265. — Signed and dated in 2d state : *Rembrandt. f.* **1656.** M. places the 1st state a year earlier.

Three states ; two shown : —
 (*a*.) 1st state in photogravure. *M. of F. A.*
 (*b*.) 2d state. *Sewall Coll.*

M. thinks that the additions in the 2d state are not by R., for which opinion he is taken to task by Mr. Haden (" Monograph," p. 51).

307. Portrait of Dr. Arnoldus Tholinx. (Pieter van Tol ; the Advocate Tolling.) — Bl 188 ; B 284 ; W 286 ; M 170 ; Du 270. — Assigned to between 1654 and 1656 by V., to 1655 by M.
Two states ; 2d state shown in photogr. *From Bl.'s R.*

308. St. Francis Praying. — Bl 78 ; B 107 ; W 112 ; M 252 ; Du 109. — Signed : *Rembrandt. f.* Dated 1657.
Two states ; 2d state shown. *Sewall Coll.*

This is one of the prints for which, according to Mr. Haden, R. adopted a background from some design by Titian or Campagnola. A remarkably fine impression, treated almost like a monotype in the wiping, is in the collection of Mr. Theodore Irwin, of Oswego, N. Y.

309. **The Presentation in the Temple.** A dark print. — Bl 23 ; B 50 ; W 55 ; M 243 ; Du 55. — Assigned to between 1656 and 1658 by V., to 1654 by M.
One state only. *Sewall Coll.*

310. **Jesus and the Samaritan Woman.** Arched. — Bl 45 ; B 70 ; W 74 ; M 253 ; Du 72. — Signed and dated in 3d state : *Rembrandt f* **1658.**
Three states ; 3d state shown. *Sewall Coll.*

M. believes the 3d state to show work by a later hand.

311. **The Woman at the Stove.** — Bl 161 ; B 197 ; W 194 ; M 299 ; Du 194. — Signed : *Rembrandt f.* Dated **1658.**
Six states ; three shown : —
   (*a.*)   2d state in photogravure. *From Bl.'s R.*
   (*b.*)   3d state. *Sewall Coll.*
   (*c.*)   6th state. *Sewall Coll.*

It has been suggested that the model which served for this and the succeeding studies of women was R.'s second wife (?), Hendrickie Jaghers or Stoffels. See, however, V., "Rembrandt," p. 358.

312. **The Bather.** — Bl 163 ; B 199 ; W 196 ; M 298 ; Du 196. — Signed : *Rembrandt. f.* Dated **1658.**
Two states ; 2d state shown. *Sewall Coll.*

313. **A Woman** with her feet in the water. — Bl 164 ; B 200 ; W 197 ; M 297 ; Du 197. — Signed : *Rembrandt f.* Dated **1658.**
One state only. *Sewall Coll.*

314. **A Woman** lying on a couch. (The Negress.) — Bl 169 ; B 205 ; W 202 ; M 300 ; Du 202. — Signed : *Rembrandt. f.* Dated **1658.**
Three states ; 3d state shown. *Sewall Coll.*

315. **Antiope and Jupiter.** — Bl 167 ; B 203 ; W 200 ; M 301 ; Du 200. — Signed : *Rembrandt. f.* Dated **1659.**
Two states ; 1st state shown. *Sewall Coll.*

316. St. Peter Healing the Cripple. (St. Peter and St. John at the Gate of the Temple.) — Bl 66; B 94; W 98; M 254; Du 97. — Signed: *Rembrandt f.* Dated 1659.

Four states; (?) state shown. *Sewall Coll.*

It is impossible, from the confused and insufficient descriptions, to make out the states of this plate. The impression shown is certainly of a later state. The wonder is that the plate is not among those classed as doubtful by the cataloguers. It is one of the worst with which R.'s name is connected. Note, for only one thing, the figure of St. John, muffled up in a cloak like the traditional Italian brigand of the stage, posed in an awkward contortion, and drawn like a bundle of clothing, without any feeling for the human figure.

317. The Landscape with the Palisades. — Bl 343; B 247; W 243; Du 244. — Dated 1659. Rejected by M. and doubted by others.

One state only. Shown in photogravure. *From Bl.'s R.*

318. The Woman with the Arrow. — Bl 166; B 202; W 199; M 302; Du 199. — Signed: *Rembradt f.* (no *n*). Dated 1661.

Three states (?); 2d (?) state shown. *Sewall Coll.*

The tinting observable in the impression shown is due to ink left upon the plate in printing. Bl. and B. describe only one state, W. describes two, M. reduces W.'s states to the rank of 2d and 3d, and describes a new 1st. This is, however, as he himself says, "a trial proof." The only difference between it and his 2d state consists in the deepening of a shadow. It is clear, therefore, that it is not "a state" at all. M. thinks that this was the last plate etched by R.

319. Portrait of Coppenol. (The Large Coppenol.) — Bl 175; B 283; W 285; M 174; Du 258. — Assigned to 1661 by V., to 1658 by M.

Six states; two shown: —

    (*a.*) 3d state.   *Gray Coll.*
    (*b.*) 6th state.   *Sewall Coll.*

See No. 77 of this catalogue.

THE FOLLOWING PIECES ARE LEFT UNCLASSIFIED BY
V. (CASES 9, 11, AND 13, 15.)

320. Three Profiles of Old Men. — Bl 303 ; B 374 ;
W 368 ; M 12 ; Du 362. — Assigned by M. to 1629.
One state only. Shown in photogravure. *From Bl.'s R.*

321. An Old Woman in a veil. — Bl 243 ; B 358 ;
W 352 ; M 68 ; Du 346. — Assigned by M. to 1631.
Two states ; 2d state shown. *Sewall Coll.*

322. A Man Grimacing. — Bl 263 ; B 308 ; W 309 ;
M 60 ; Du 304. — Assigned by M. to 1631.
Three states ; 2d state shown. *Sewall Coll.*

All but the 1st state probably retouched by a later hand, according
to M.

323. Head of a Man, small, with a grotesque hat.
(Slave with a High Hat.) — Bl 296 ; B 302 ; W 302 ;
M 81 ; Du 298. — Assigned by M. to 1631.
Two states ; 2d state shown. *Sewall Coll.*

324. An Old Man, with white beard, and fur cap. —
Bl 278 ; B 312 ; W 313 ; M 64 ; Du 308. — Assigned by M.
to 1631.
Two states ; 2d state shown. *Sewall Coll.*

325. An Old Man, with head bowed down. — Bl 300 ;
B 296 ; W 296 ; M 95 ; Du 292. — Assigned by M. to
·1632.
One state only. *Sewall Coll.*

326. An Elderly Man, with his underlip thrust out. —
Bl 259 ; B 305 ; W 305 ; M 119 ; Du 301. — Assigned to
1635 by M.
Two states ; 1st state shown. *Sewall Coll.*

V. thinks this piece " very doubtful."

327. **The Large Tree beside the House.** Morning effect. — Bl 310 ; B 207 ; W 204; M 303 ; Du 204. — Assigned by M. to 1640.
One state only.   Shown in photogravure.   *From Bl.'s R.*

328. **The Draughtsman.** — Bl 100 ; B 130 ; W 133 ; M 270 ; Du 130. — Assigned by M. to 1641.
Two states ; 1st state shown.   *Sewall Coll.*

329. **An Old Woman Reading.** — Bl 248 ; B 362 ; W 356 ; M 149 ; Du 350. — Assigned by M. to 1641.
One state only.   Shown in photogravure.   *From Bl.'s R.*

330. **A Young Man,** wearing a hat. — Bl 256 ; B 330 ; W 327 ; M 163 ; Du 322. — Assigned by M. to 1651.
One state only.   Shown in photogravure.   *From Bl.'s R.*

331. **Sketches** of a horse, a grove, etc. — Bl 348 ; B 364 ; W 358 ; M 166 ; Du 352. — Assigned by M. to 1652.
One state only.   Shown in photogravure.   *From Bl.'s R.*

332. **An Elderly Man,** wearing a cap with earflaps. — Bl 295 ; B 323 ; W 321 ; Du 316. — Rejected by M.
One state only.   Shown in photogravure.   *From Bl.'s R.*

333. **An Old Man,** with a pointed beard. — Bl 306 ; W 334. — Rejected by M.
One state only.   *Not procurable.*

Although Bl. describes this piece, he nevertheless also rejects it.

334. **Head of a Man,** with curly hair. — Bl 307 ; W 336. — Rejected by M.
One state only.   *Not procurable.*

This again Bl. describes, but nevertheless rejects.

335. **The Landscape with the Little Man.** — Bl 339 ; B 239 ; W 237 ; Du 237. — Rejected by M.
One state only.   *Not procurable.*

Rejected by Bl. also, although he describes it.

336. A Landscape, with a fisherman in a boat. — Bl 341 ; B 243 ; W 239 ; Du 240. — Rejected by M.
One state only. Shown in photogravure. *From Bl.'s R.*

337. The Village Street. — Bl 347 ; B 254 ; W 250 ; Du 251. — Rejected by M.
One state only. Shown in photogravure. *From Bl.'s R.*

Bl. is inclined to think that this is the work of a child, perhaps of Titus.

338. An Old Man, in a cap. — Bl 304.
One state only. Shown in photogravure. *From Bl.'s R.*

Described by Bl. only, and doubted by him.

339. An Old Man, in a fur cap. — Bl 305.
One state only. Shown in photogravure. *From Bl.'s R.*

Like No. 338, described by Bl. only, and doubted by him.

THE FOLLOWING PIECES ARE EITHER EXPLICITLY REJECTED BY V., OR TACITLY OMITTED BY HIM. (CASES 17, 19.)

340. Rembrandt. — Bl 230; B 338 ; W 30 ; M 7 ; Du 30. — Monogram apparently *RHL.* Dated **1629.** The whole reversed.
One state only. Shown in photogravure. *From Bl.'s R.*

341. A Philosopher with an hour-glass. — Bl 113 ; B 318; W 318 ; M 15 ; Du 313. — R H **1630,** said to be on 2d state.
Two (or three ?) states ; (?) state shown. *Sewall Coll.*

The impression shown does not agree with any of the descriptions of states, neither do the reproductions given by Bl. and by Du. As this is evidently surface printing, *i. e.*, printing from a relief block cut either on wood or on metal, some queer " plugging " must have been done for the pleasure of manufacturing the various states described.

342. The Onion Woman. — Bl 102 ; B 134 ; M 66 ;
Du 133. — Marked in 2d state : Rt 1631. `
Two states ; 2d state shown.   *Sewall Coll.*

M. does " not hesitate to attribute this print to R." The monogram
and date have little of the character of those seen on undoubted
works.

343. A Young Man wearing a cap. — Bl 297 ; B 322 ;
W 320 ; M 46 ; Du 315. — Marked in 1st state : RH 1631.
Two states ; 2d state shown in photogr.   *From Bl.'s R.*

344. An Old Man with square beard and high forehead. — Bl 279 ; B 314 ; W 315 ; M 59 ; Du 310. — Assigned
by M. to 1631.
Two states ; 2d state shown in photogr.   *From Bl.'s R.*

345. An Elderly Man with a bushy beard. — Bl 277 ;
B 297 ; W 297 ; M 61 ; Du 293. — Monogram apparently
RH. Dated 1631.
Three states ; 2d state shown in photogr. *From Bl.'s R.*

346. Rembrandt's Mother in widow's dress. — Bl.
197 ; B 344 ; W 340 ; M 92 ; Du 333. — Signed : *Rembrandt.f.*
Assigned by M to 1632.
One state only.   *Sewall Coll.*

**347. Jacob Lamenting the Supposed Death of
Joseph.** — Bl 10 ; B 38 ; W 42 ; M 189 ; Du 42. — *Rem-
brant* (no *d*) *van Rijn ft.*   Assigned to 1633 by M.
One state only.   *Sewall Coll.*

M. thinks this plate may possibly be by Van Vliet. The signature
is certainly peculiar. " It only occurs once again in these etchings,"
says M., ". . . the larger Resurrection of Lazarus." This, however,
is not strictly true, as the comparison will show. See No. 69 of this
catalogue.

348. Two Travelling Peasants. — Bl 110 ; B 144 ;
W 144 ; M 104 ; Du 142. — Assigned by M. to 1634.
One state only.   *Sewall Coll.*

349. **Philosopher in Meditation.** — Bl 112 ; B 148 ; W 146 ; M 276 ; Du 144. — Assigned by. M. to 1642.
Five states ; 3d state shown. *Sewall Coll.*

There is a pretty close copy of this print in the Sewall Collection. No copies are mentioned by M.

350. **Female Peasant** holding a jug. — Bl 144 ; B 181 ; W 178 ; Du 177. — Attributed to Lievens by M.
One state only. Shown in photogravure. *From Bl.'s R.*

351. **Male Peasant** with a basket by his side. — Bl 143 ; B 180 ; W 177 ; Du 176. — Attributed to Lievens by M.
One state only. *Sewall Coll.*

352. **A Young Woman**, reading. — Bl 247 ; B 361 ; W 355 ; Du 349. — Rejected by M.
One state only. *Not procurable.*

Rejected also by Bl., although he describes it.

353. **A Young Man** in a turned-up hat. — Bl 254 ; B 329 ; W 326 ; Du 321. — Rejected by M.
Two states ; 2d state shown in photogr. *From Bl.'s R.*

354. **The Big Tree.** — Bl 340 ; B 241 ; W 238 ; Du 238. — Rejected by M.
One state only. Shown in photogravure. *From Bl.'s R.*

355. **A Cottage with a Barn filled with Hay.** — Bl 344 ; B 248 ; W 244 ; Du 245. — Rejected by M.
One state only. Shown in photogravure. *From Bl.'s R.*

356. **The Mother of Rembrandt.** — Bl 194 ; B 353 ; Du 342.
States (?). *Not procurable.*

This plate is described by the older cataloguers, and after them by some of the later. No impressions, however, can now be found, and it is a question whether the plate ever existed. This is only one of several similar cases.

357. Portrait of Jan Six. — Bl 185.
Two states (?).   2d (?) state, shown in photogravure.
                                                     From Bl.'s R.
Described only by Bl.

358.   The Nail Cutter.   (Bathseba.) — B 127.
One state only.   *Sewall Coll.*

Described only by B.   Rejected by all later writers.

359.   Cupid. — B 132.
One state only.   *Sewall Coll.*

Described only by B.   Rejected by all later writers.

360.   The Hour of Death. — B 108.
Two states ; 2d state shown.   *Gray Coll.*

Attributed to Ferdinand Bol by all later writers.

361.   The Pen Cutter. — Daulby 361.
States (?).   *Sewall Coll.*

This piece is attributed to R. by Daulby, but rejected by all other
writers.

ETCHINGS, ENGRAVINGS, ETC.

EXECUTED FROM PAINTINGS AND SKETCHES BY REM-
BRANDT.   (CASES 30–39, 20–25, AND 27.)

The following etchings, etc., are arranged chonologi-
cally, in the order of the years in which R. executed, or is
supposed to have executed, the originals which they trans-
late.   It has been impossible, however, to exhibit them in
the order of the catalogue, owing to considerations of size,
etc.   For this reason the case number is given after each
title, which will enable the visitor to find any given number
without difficulty.   Cases 30 to 39 are in the southern half
of the room, cases 20 to 25, and 27 in the northern half.

362. St. Paul in Prison. (Case 20.) — Dated 1627.
— Museum at Stuttgart. — Etched by N. Baldinger.
S. R. Koehler.

The earliest known dated picture by R. Compare No. 54 of this catalogue.

363. The Money Changer. (Case 20.) — Dated
1627. — Berlin, Gallery. — Etched by Wm. Unger.
S. R. Koehler.

Not catalogued by V. See Dr. W. Bode, " Rembrandt's früheste Thätigkeit," in " Graphische Künste," Vol. III, p. 49 *et seq.*

364. St. Jerome in a Grotto. (Case 20.) — Assigned to about 1629 to 1630 by V. —Berlin, Gallery.—
Etched by J. J. Van Vliet in 1631. (Shown in photogravure.) *S. R. Koehler.*

365. Hermit (or Loth ?) in a Grotto. (Anchises
at the burning of Troy.) (Case 20.) — Dated 1630. —
Cesar Collection (in Schmidt's time). — Etched by G. F.
Schmidt. *Gray Coll.*

366. Portrait of an Old Man. (Case 20.) — Dated
1630. — Cassel Gallery. — Etched by Wm. Unger. ·
S. R. Koehler.

367. The Entombment of Christ. (Case 20.) —
Dated 1630. — British Museum. — Heliotype.
S. R. Koehler.

See No. 69 of this catalogue.

368. Loth and his Daughters. (Case 20.) — Dated
1631. — Etched by J. J. Van Vliet. (Shown in photogravure.) *S. R. Koehler.*

See the original etching under No. 432.

369. **Loth and his Daughters.** (Case 20.) — Assigned to about 1631 by V. — Collection of Prince Henry of Prussia (in Schmidt's time). — Etched by G. F. Schmidt.   *Gray Coll.*

370. **The Baptism of the Eunuch.** (Case 21.) — Assigned to about 1631 by V. — Etched by J. J. Van Vliet in 1631. (Shown in photogravure.)   *S. R. Koehler.*

371. **Holy Family.** (Case 21.) — Dated 1631. — Munich, Pinakothek. — Etched by P. Halm.   *S. R. Koehler.*

Not catalogued by V. See Dr. W. Bode, as under No. 363.

372. **Dr. Nicolas Tulp's Anatomical Lecture.** (Case 30.) — Dated 1632. — The Hague, Museum. — Etched by J. P. de Frey.   *Gray Coll.*

372A. **The Same.** (Case 21.) — Etched by Wm. Unger.   *S. R. Koehler.*

373. **Maurits Huygens,** Secretary of the Council of State. (Case 21.) — Dated 1632. — Hamburg, Wesselhœft Collection. — Etched by W. Hecht.   *S. R. Koehler.*

374. **Study of the Head of an Old Man.** (Case 38.) — Dated 1632. Oldenburg, Gallery. — Etched by L. Kühn.   *S. R. Koehler.*

Not catalogued by V. See Dr. W. Bode, "Bilderlese aus kleineren Gemäldesammlungen," Vienna: 1885, etc.

375. **Portrait of a Young Dutch Woman.** (Case 21.) — Dated 1632. — Vienna, Academical Gallery. — Etched by Wm. Unger.   ·   *S. R. Koehler.*

Not catalogued by V. See "Zeitschrift für bildende Kunst," Vol. XIII, p. 224.

376. **Philosopher in Contemplation.** (Case 30.) — Dated 1633. — Paris, Louvre. — Engraved by Caronni and Longhi.   *Gray Coll.*

377. Philosopher in Meditation. (Case 31.) —
Dated 1633. — Paris, Louvre. — Engraved by Cozzi and
Longhi. Gray Coll.

378. Man Studying. (Case 21.) — Dated 1633. —
Brunswick, Gallery. — Etched by Wm. Unger.
S. R. Koehler.

Dr. W. Bode, "Zeitschrift für bildende Kunst," Vol. V, p. 175, reads
the date, which is injured, 1633. V. assigns the picture to about 1645.

379. Saskia Smiling. (Rembrandt's Daughter.)
(Case 31.) — Dated 1633. — Dresden, Gallery. — Lithogr.
by Hanfstängl. Gray Coll.

It is hardly necessary to say that the second title is erroneous. In
1633 R. was himself only twenty-six years old.

380. Portrait of a Gentleman. (Borgomastro
Olandese.) (Case 32.) — Dated 1633. — Casa Mamfrini
(in 1811). — Engraved by G. Longhi. Gray Coll.

381. Saskia, R.'s Wife. (Case 21.) — Dated 1633.
Berlin, Print Cabinet. — Etched by Wm. Unger.
S. R. Koehler.

Silverpoint drawing on parchment. See about the curious discrep-
ancy in the date, V., " Rembrandt," 2d ed., pp. 132 and 133, and
"American Art Review," Vol. II, Div. 2, pp. 112-114.

382. The Shipbuilder and His Wife. (Case 32.)
— Dated 1633. — Buckingham Palace. — Mezzot. by C.
H. Hodges. Sewall Coll.

383. Portrait of an Old Lady. (Case 21.) — Dated
1634. — London, National Gallery. — Etched by Paul
Rajon. S. R. Koehler.

384. Rembrandt. (Count Horn.) (Case 21.) —
Dated 1634. — Florence, Pitti Palace. — Etched by G. F.
Schmidt. Gray Coll.

See No. 471.

385. **Young Lady with Flowers.** (Saskia.) (Case
22.) — Dated 1634. — St. Petersburg, Hermitage. —
Etched by N. Massaluff.   *S. R. Koehler.*

386. **Samson Threatening his Father-in-Law.**
(Duke Adolphus of Guelders threatening his father.)
(Case 22.) — Date read **1635** by V. — Berlin, Gallery. —
Etched by G. F. Schmidt.   *Gray Coll.*

387. **Tobias and His Wife.** (Case 22.) — Assigned to about 1635 to 1640 by V. — Etched by G. F.
Schmidt.   *Gray Coll.*

388. **A Warrior (Officer).** (Case 33.) — Dated
1635. — Cambridge, Fitz-William College. — Mezzot. by
Wm. Pether.   *Gray Coll.*

389. **Repose During the Flight to Egypt.** (Case
22.) — Assigned to about 1635 to 1636 by V. — Berlin,
Gallery. — Etched by Leopold Flameng.   *S. R. Koehler.*

390. **Winter Landscape.** (Case 22.) — Assigned
to 1636 by V. — Cassel, Gallery. — Etched by Wm. Unger.   *S. R. Koehler.*

Signature and date forged, according to V., who, however, accepts
the picture, and assigns it as stated.

391. **Rembrandt and Saskia.** (Case 22.) — Dated
1638.— Dresden, Gallery. — Etched by H. Bürkner.
                                          S. R. Koehler.

392. **The Marriage Feast of Samson.** (The
Feast of Ahasuerus.) (Case 34.) — Dated **1638**. — Dresden, Gallery. — Lithograph by Hanfstängl.   *Gray Coll.*

393. **Portrait of a Gentleman.** (Burgomaster Six.)
— (Case 22.) — Dated **1639**. — Cassel, Gallery. — Etched
by Wm. Unger.   *S. R. Koehler.*

It is self-evident that the second title is erroneous. Compare No.
243.

394. Portrait of the Artist Doomer (?). (The Gilder.) (Case 22.) — Dated **1640.** — Wm. Schaus, New York. — Etched by Leopold Flameng. *S. R. Koehler.*

V. points out that the traditional title, " Le Doreur," is probably a corruption, or misreading, of the name of the person represented.

395. Portrait of a Lady. (Case 22.) — About 1640(?). — Budapest, Gallery. — Etched by L. Michalek. *S. R. Koehler.*

Not catalogued by V. See Tschudy and Pulsky, "Landes-Gemälde-Gallerie in Budapest," Vienna, 1883 and 1886, Part II, p. 9.

396. Manoah's Sacrifice. (Case 34.) — Dated **1641.** — Dresden, Gallery. — Engraved by Jacob Houbraken. *Sewall Coll.*

397. The Jewish Bride. (Saskia.) (Case 23.) — Dated **1641.** — Vienna, Coll. of Count Lanckoroncki. — Etched by G. F. Schmidt. *Gray Coll.*

Schmidt's etching is reversed. This picture has been doubted. See Dr. W. Bode, in " Mittheilungen der Gesellschaft für vervielfältigende Kunst," Vienna, Vol. III, No. 3, May 15, 1875, pp. 38 and 39. Also ' American Art Review," Vol. II, Div. 2, p. 114.

397A. The Same. (Case 23.) Etched by Wm. Unger. *S. R. Koehler.*

398. Banning Cock's Company Sallying Forth to Shoot. (The Nightwatch.) (Case 33.) — Dated **1642.** — Amsterdam, Museum. — Etched by Leopold Flameng. *Sewall Coll.*

399. An Old Man Seated. (Case 37.) — Dated **1642.** — Budapest, Gallery. — Etched by Wm. Unger. *S. R. Koehler.*

Not catalogued by V. See Tschudy and Pulsky, "Landes-Gemälde-Gallerie in Budapest," Vienna, 1883 and 1886, Part II, p. 8.

400. Le Connetable de Bourbon? (Case 23.) — Dated **1644.** — Paris, M. Secrétan (according to Dutuit). — Dry-point by Ch. Kœpping. (Part only of the picture?)   *S. R. Kœhler.*

401. Eleazar Swalm. (Case 35.) — Assigned to 1645 by V. — Where? — Engraved by Jonas Suyderhoef. *Sewall Coll.*

- **402. Portrait of an Elderly Man.** (A Jewish Rabbi.) (Case 23.) — Dated **1645.** — Berlin, Gallery (from the Suermondt Coll.). — Etched by Leopold Flameng.   *S. R. Koehler.*

403. The Descent from the Cross. (The Crucifixion.) (Case 35.) — Assigned to about 1645 to 1650 by V. — London, National Gallery. — Engraved by J. Burnet. *Sewall Coll.*

404. Holy Family. (The family of the Woodchopper, or of the Carpenter.) (Case 23.) — Dated **1646.** — Cassel, Gallery. — Etched by Wm. Unger. *S. R. Koehler.*

405. An Aged Rabbi. (Case 38.) — Dated **1646.** — Where? — Mezzotint by Capt. Wm. Baillie.   *Gray Coll.*

406. Nicolas Berchem. (Case 24.) — Dated **1647.** — Grosvenor House. — Engraved by Schiavonetti. *Sewall Coll.*

407. Landscape with Ruins. (Case 25.) — Assigned to about 1643 to 1650 by V. — Cassel, Gallery. — Etched by Wm. Unger.   *S. R. Koehler.*

407A. The Student. (Daniel Studying Chaldaic?) (Case 24.) — About 1647 to 1650? — Berlin, Mr. Otto Pein. — Photogravure.   *S. R. Koehler.*

This picture is not mentioned by V., as it has come to light only lately. Note some of R.'s studio property in it, the sword which occurs in the "Resurrection of Lazarus" (No. 69), and a chair like that in "The Death of the Virgin" (No. 164). See Adolph Rosenberg in "Zeitschrift für bildende Kunst," Vol. XXII, pp. 163 and 164.

408. A Jewish Rabbi. (Framed, on case.) — Dated 1651. — London, National Gallery. — Etched by Chas. Waltner. *Edward Robinson.*

V. is quite explicit in giving the date, but no date is mentioned in the official catalogue of the National Gallery.

409. Noli me tangere. (Case 25.) — Dated 1651. — Brunswick, Gallery. — Etched by Wm. Unger. *S. R. Koehler.*

410. Portrait of a Lady. (Case 38.) — Assigned to between 1650 and 1654 by V. — Paris, Louvre. — Etched by Ch. Koepping. *Sewall Coll.*

Dr. W. Bode is inclined to assign this picture to 1658. See Dutuit Supplement, p. 35.

411. An Old Man with a Cane. (Case 24.) — Assigned to 1654 by V. — Dresden, Gallery. — Etched by N. Massaloff. *S. R. Koehler.*

412. The Standard Bearer. (Case 25.) — Assigned to 1655 by V. — Cassel, Gallery. Engraved by E. Heinemann. *S. R. Koehler.*

413. The Standard Bearer. (Case 36.) — Date? — Where? — Mezzot. by Wm. Pether. *Gray Coll.*

This picture is placed here, as V. mentions two "Standard Bearers," the second in the Collection J. de Rothschild, Paris. The description, however, does not fit, nor does Pether's mezzotint show R.'s character.

414. Jacob Blessing the Sons of Joseph. (Case 25.) — Dated 1656. — Cassel, Gallery. — Engraved by E. Heinemann. *S. R. Koehler.*

415. Mountainous Landscape with a Torrent. (Case 25.) — Assigned to 1656 by V. — Brunswick, Gallery. — Etched by Wm. Unger. *S. R. Koehler.*

416. Rembrandt. (Case 39.) — Assigned to 1658 by V. — Vienna, Belvedere. — Etched by Wm. Unger.
S. R. Koehler.

417. The Auctioneer. (Thomas Jacobsz. Haring ?) (Case 25.) — Dated **1658.** — London, Mr. John Wilson. — Etched by Wm. Unger. *S. R. Koehler.*

418. Rembrandt. (Case 36.) — Dated **1659.** — Coll. of Lord Carrington (in 1842). — Mezzot. by Richard Earlom. *Gray Coll.*

419. The Syndics of the Cloth Hall. (Case 25.) — Dated **1661.** — Amsterdam, Museum. — Etched by G. F. Schmidt. *Sewall Coll.*

Schmidt's etching is reversed.

419A. The Same. (Case 25.) — Etched by Wm. Unger. *S. R. Koehler.*

420. A Family Group. (Rembrandt's Family.) (Case 27.) — Assigned to about 1662 to 1663 by V. — Brunswick, Gallery. — Etched by Wm. Unger.
S. R. Koehler.

Again it goes without saying that the second title is quite unwarranted. W. Bürger, " Zeitschrift für bildende Kunst," Vol. IV, p. 102, assigns the picture to the period after 1665.

. **421. Lucretia.** (Case 39.) — Dated **1664.** — Was in the San Donato Collection. — Etched by Ch. Koepping.
Sewall Coll.

422. Rembrandt. (Case 27.) — Assigned to 1668 by V. — Florence, Pitti Palace. — Etched by J. G. Chapman. *S. R. Koehler.*

423. Jewish Rabbi. (Case 37.) — Date ? — Where ? — Mezzot. by Wm. Pether. *Gray Coll.*

424. Sigismond Ragotsky ? (Case 39.) — Date ? — Where ? — Mezzot. by Bernard Picart. *Sewall Coll.*

[425. **Christ Blessing the Children.** — National Gallery, London. From the Suermondt Collection. — Etched by Leopold Flameng. *S. R. Koehler.*

In the 1st edition of his " Rembrandt," V. assigns this picture to about 1650. In the 2d edition (p. 285) he rejects it, and names as its probable author either Victor or Eeckhout.]

ETCHINGS

EXECUTED BY ARTISTS BELONGING TO REMBRANDT'S CIRCLE.

PIETER LASTMAN. (CASE 12.)

Born (at Amsterdam?) about 1580 to 1584 ; died (in the same city?) about 1649. Lastman was R.'s last teacher. — See Vosmær, "Rembrandt," 2d ed., Chap. VIII, and pp. 472 to 481.

426. **Judah and Thamar.** — Bartsch, Rembr. Cat., II, p. 133, No. 74.
Two states ; 2d state shown. . *Gray Coll.*

Possibly only after Lastman. See Vosmær, p. 79.

SALOMON SAVRY. (CASE 12.)

Engraver and etcher, who is said to have worked at Amsterdam from 1620 to 1650. As early as 1632, in the year, that is to say, which is marked upon the original, he copied R.'s " Ratkiller," No. 72 of this catalogue (Vosmær, p. 99). Mr. Haden, " Monograph." p. 18, would have it that he etched also the two plates, Nos. 95 and 96 of this catalogue, generally believed to be by R. — See Andresen, " Handbuch," I, p. 437.

427. Cornelis Claesz. Anslo. — Copy of R.'s etching, No. 206 of this catalogue.   Attributed to Savry by B.

Sewall Coll.

428. The Good Samaritan. — Copy of R.'s etching, No. 80 of this catalogue.   Attributed to Savry by W.

Sewall Coll.

Both these plates are marked S. Savry excud. (cut off in the " Samaritan "), but this in reality signifies only that they were published by him.

SALOMON KONINCK. (CASE 12.)

Born at Amsterdam 1609, died about 1668. A pupil of N. Moeijart, who adopted R.'s style. (Not to be confounded with Philip de Koninck, one of R.'s own pupils.) — See Vosmær, pp. 63 and 97 ; Bartsch's Rembr. Catalogue, II ; Claussin, Supplement.

429. Bust of an Old Man in Profile. — Bartsch, Rembr. Cat., II, p. 130, 68 ; Claussin, Supplement, p. 132, 75.

One state only.   *Sewall Coll.*

According to B. and to Cl., this plate is signed and dated *S. Koninck Ao.* **1628,** which does not quite correspond with what is left of the inscription on the impression shown, viz.: AN 1628. The name has evidently been cut off. Judging from the date, this plate must have been executed before K. was influenced by R.

M. RODDERMONDT. (CASE 12.)

(Rodermont, Rodermondt, Rottermondt ; called also Aegidius Paul, or Paul Aegidius, R.) Dutch painter and etcher, who is said to have worked about 1640. Mr. Haden ("Monograph," pp. 17, 18, and 26) would make him responsible for some of R.'s work.

430. **Esau selling his Birthright to Jacob.** — Bartsch, Rembr. Cat., II, p. 135, 77 ; Claussin, Suppl., p. 135, 84.
Two states ; 2d state shown. *Sewall Coll.*

Mr. Haden refers to this plate, "Monograph," p. 18. The false signature, "Rembrandt," does not occur in the first state.

431. **The Suppliant.** — Bartsch, Rembr. Cat., II, p. 137, 78 ; Claussin, Suppl., p. 136, 85.
One state only. *Sewall Coll.*

JAN JORIS VAN VLIET. (CASE 14.)

Born at Delft, in 1610, painter and etcher. "Van Vliet is especially known," says Vosmær, p. 99, "by his etchings after Rembrandt. He was the first who made it his aim to reproduce the works of the young master." — See Bartsch, Rembr. Cat., II ; Claussin, Supplement ; also Mr. Haden, "Monograph," pp. 14, 15, 24, 25.

432. **Loth and his Daughters.** After Rembrandt. — B 1 ; Cl 1. — Dated 1631.
Two states ; 2d state shown. *Sewall Coll.*

433. **Susannah and the Elders.** After Jan Lievens. — B 3 ; Cl 3.
One state only. *Sewall Coll.*

The impression shown has been cut, mounted and repaired.

434. **Old Woman Reading.** After Rembrandt. — B 18; Cl 18.
One state only. *Sewall Coll.*

435. **The Seller of Ratsbane.** — B 55 ; Cl 55.
One state only. *Sewall Coll.*

436. The Beggars. — B 73–82 ; Cl 73–82.
One state only.   *Sewall Coll.*

The set here shown lacks two of the full series of ten.
See also Nos. 364 and 370.

FERDINAND BOL. (CASES 16 AND 18.)

Born at Dordrecht towards 1611, but lived in Amsterdam since
childhood; died at Amsterdam, 1681.   Rembrandt is named as his only
master.   See Vosmær, pp. 138 and 139; Bartsch, Rembr. Cat. II;
Claussin, Supplement; also Mr. Haden, " Monograph," p. 15 and elsewhere.

437. The Sacrifice of Abraham. — B 1 ; Cl 1.
Two states ; 2d state shown.   *Sewall Coll.*

438. Gideon's Sacrifice. — B 2 ; Cl 2.
Three states ; 3d (?) state shown.   *Sewall Coll.*

439. St. Jerome. — B 3 ; Cl 3.
One state only.   *Sewall Coll.*

There seems no reason to think that this is not the etching described
by B. and by Cl.   Nevertheless it measures only 8 pouces 4 lignes across,
while they agree in making it 9 pouces.

440. The Family. — B 4 ; Cl 4. — Dated 1649.
One state only.   *Sewall Coll.*

441. An Old Man with a curly beard. — B 9 ; Cl
9. — Dated 1642.
One state only.   *Sewall Coll.*

Traces only of the signature and date are visible on the impression
shown.

442. Portrait of an Officer. — B 11 ; Cl 12.
One state only.   *Gray Coll.*

443. Portrait of a Man. — B 12 ; Cl 13.
One state only.   *Sewall Coll.*

444. Man Wearing a Large Cap. — B 13 ; Cl 14.
Oen state only. *Sewall Coll.*

445. The Woman with the Pear. — B 14 ; Cl 16.
— Dated **1651**.
One state only. *Gray Coll.*

446. Portrait of a Lady, in an oval. — B 15 ; Cl 17.
— Dated **1644**.
Two states ; 2d state shown. *Sewall Coll.*

The impression shown is not the original, but the copy made by
Claussin. The original is a trifle larger, and the copper in the 2d state
has been cut to an oval shape.

447. Bust of an Old Man, in an oval. — Cl 18.
One state only. *Sewall Coll.*

448. The Hour of Death. — B (under Rembrandt)
108 ; Cl 19.

Exhibited among the pieces eliminated by V. from the list of R.'s
works. See No. 360 of this catalogue, in case 17, 19.

449. Young Man Standing. — Signed, and dated
1640.
States (?). *Gray Coll.*

Not mentioned in any of the catalogues, and not at all like Bol's
work. The same design has been etched by some one else, and signed
Rembrandt f. 1636. An impression of this version is also shown.

JAN LIEVENS. (CASES 26 AND 28.)

Born at Leyden, 1607. It is generally stated that he died at Antwerp in 1663, but in 1672 he was still living, and again in his native
city. Lievens, like R., was a pupil of Lastman, and only a follower of
his greater townsman. About 1634 he was at Antwerp, and later his
style was influenced by Rubens and the Italians. See Vosmær, p. 97,
and elsewhere; Bartsch, Rembr. Cat., II; Claussin, Supplement. For
Mr. Haden's theories concerning Lievens, see " Monograph," p. 16
and elsewhere.

450. The Virgin and Child. — Bl 1 ; Cl 1.
Two states ; 1st state shown.   *Sewall Coll.*

This is evidently in L.'s later Italian, or "noble " manner.

451. The Resurrection of Lazarus. — B 3 ; Cl 3.
Two states ; 2d state shown.   *Sewall Coll.*

452. St. Jerome. — B 5; Cl 5.
Three states; 2d state shown.   *Sewall Coll.*

453. An Hermit. (St. Francis.) — B 7 ; Cl 7.
Two states ; 2d state shown.   *Sewall Coll.*

454. St. Anthony. — B 8 ; Cl 8.
Two states ; 2d state shown.   *Sewall Coll.*

This is an extreme case of the attempted free use of the graver, on a plate apparently underbitten, often met with in L.'s work. R. evidently used the graver upon his plates in a most skilful manner, and with a dexterity and freedom that made it harmonize admirably with the work of the acid and the dry-point. His follower attempts the same thing, but, lacking the skill, the freedom degenerates into brutality.

455. Oriental Figure. — B 12 ; Cl 12.
Two states ; 2d state shown.   *Sewall Coll.*

In this plate the retouches were etched in, but with as little success as in the case of the retouches put in with the graver.

456. Bust of an Oriental. — B 13 ; Cl 13.
Two states ; 2d state shown.   *Sewall Coll.*

The curious crayon-like texture noticeable in this plate may be due to shallow biting and lines run together, or in parts, as Mr. Jas. D. Smillie suggests, to the grinding down of heavily overbitten lines.

457. Bust of an Oriental. — B 18 ; Cl 18.
Two states ; 2d (?) state shown.   *Sewall Coll.*

Both B. and Cl. say that L.'s initials are to be seen on the left side, about midway, but they are not to be found in this impression. See R.'s etching, No. 116 of this catalogue, of which this plate is supposed to be a reversed copy. See also Mr. Haden's remarks, "Monograph," pp. 28 and 29.

458. Bust of an Old Man. — B 22 ; Cl 22.
Two states (?); 1st state (?) shown. *Sewall Coll.*

B. and Cl. describe only one state, with F. van Wyngaerde's address.
As there is no address on this impression, it would seem to be a 1st
state. Or is it a copy, since it is numbered 4 in upper right-hand
corner, as if it belonged to a series?

459. Bust of a Young Man. — B 26 ; Cl 26.
One state only. *Sewall Coll.*

The breadth of the impression shown does not correspond with the
descriptions, but it has evidently been cut. Compare No. 125 of the
present catalogue, of which this is supposed to be a free copy.

460. Bust of a Young Woman. — B 27; Cl 27.
One state only. *Sewall Coll.*

This impression has likewise been cut.

461. Bust of a Young Man. — B 39 ; Cl 39.
Two states ; 2d state shown. *Sewall Coll.*

462. Head of an Old Man. — B 46 ; Cl 46.
One state only. *Sewall Coll.*

Of L.'s later time, after he had gone to Antwerp? The stippling in
this head reminds one of the similar treatment adopted by Van Dyck.

463. Bust of an Old Man, with large round eyes. —
B 50 ; Cl 50.
Two states ; 1st state shown. *Sewall Coll.*

464. Portrait of Ephraim Bonus. — B 56 ; Cl 55.
Three states ; 1st state shown. *Sewall Coll.*

Finished with free graver work, like the others of L.'s large portraits,
but much more successfully and carefully than the St. Anthony. See
R.'s portrait of Bonus, No. 244 of this catalogue.

465. Portrait of Justus Vondel. — B 57 ; Cl 56.
Five states; 4th state shown. *Sewall Coll.*

466. Portrait of Daniel Heinsius. — B 58 ; Cl 57.
One state only.   *Sewall Coll.*

467. Portrait of Jacob Gouters. — B 59 ; Cl 58.
One state only.   *Gray Coll.*

468. Bust of an Old Man, full face. — Cl 70.
One state only.   *Sewall Coll.*

The measurements do not agree. Cl. says 9 pouces by 8. The true measurement (unless this should be a copy, which is not likely) is 10 pouces 2 lignes by 8, from platemark to platemark. See the remarks about graver work under No. 454.

PAINTINGS.

469. Danae and Jupiter? — Signed and dated **1652**.
Francis Brooks.

The title hardly suits the picture. The male figure is Mercury. The woman to whom he offers the bag cannot be Danaë, as the scene takes place in the open air, while the mother of Perseus was kept by her father in a subterranean room, through the roof of which Jupiter entered in the form of a shower of gold. R., however, was evidently not a strict interpreter of ancient myths. In the etching, No. 33 of this catalogue, he introduces the shower of gold and the satyr, thus combining the two myths of Danaë and of Antiope. The picture is not mentioned by V. See also the remarks in the introduction.

470. Rembrandt? — Date? — Original where?
Boston Athenæum.
Copy by an unknown artist.

471. Rembrandt. — Dated 1634. — Original in the Pitti Palace, Florence.   *Boston Athenæum.*

Copy by an unknown artist. See G. F. Schmidt's etching, reversed, No. 384 of this catalogue.

FINDING LIST

FOR THE CATALOGUES OF BLANC, BARTSCH, WILSON, MIDDLETON, AND DUTUIT.

To locate in this exhibition by means of the following list any of Rembrandt's etchings, according to the numbers given to them by Bl, B, W, M, or Du, find the corresponding number in the first column. The number on the same line with it, in the column set apart for the catalogue used, will be the number under which the etching sought is here catalogued. For instance: the etching wanted being B 225, find this number in the first column, then read the number on the same line with it in the column headed B, which in this case is 211, and under this number the etching looked for will be found in the present catalogue. The numbers omitted indicate prints which are omitted also in this catalogue, because they are not procurable, and are described by neither V. nor Bl.

	Bl	B	W	M	Du		Bl	B	W	M	Du
1	156	25	25	128	25	24	6	23	23	26	23
2	305	101	101	126	101	25	79	61	61	27	61
3	152	88	88	5	88	26	275	161	161	31	161
4	157	29	29	75	29	27	182	31	31	23	31
5	227	30	30	4	30	28	286	156	68	14	68
6	298	87	87	3	87	29	287	305	27	22	27
7	196	59	59	340	59	30	183	152	340	20	340
8	296	102	102	258	102	31	228	—	67	21	67
9	158	65	65	257	65	32	198	—	232	123	232
10	347	24	24	9	24	33	173	157	26	185	26
11	90	295	295	255	295	34	288	227	89	12	89
12	171	66	66	320	66	35	289	298	156	189	156
13	278	28	28	254	28	36	279	296	305	16	305
14	274	63	63	129	63	37	8	158	152	10	152
15	273	62	62	341	62	38	290	347	227	15	157
16	197	60	60	66	60	39	280	90	298	17	227
17	91	86	86	87	86	40	170	171	296	19	298
18	285	104	104	—	104	41	80	278	158	18	158
19	181	149	149	30	149	42	108	273	347	29	347
20	284	160	160	67	160	43	143	197	90	89	90
21	7	167	167	65	167	44	107	91	171	63	278
22	163	253	253	28	253	45	310	285	278	60	273
23	309	105	105	24	105	46	92	181	273	343	197

Bl	B	W	M	Du		Bl	B	W	M	Du
47....214	284	274	68	296		100.....328	94	—	88	109
48.....69	7	197	62	171		101......168	71	229	85	199
49....269	163	91	61	91		102.....342	110	109	121	164
50....297	309	285	102	285		103......44	216	199	176	94
51....299	6	181	25	181		104.....209	259	167	348	71
52....144	79	284	59	284		105......74	217	94	104	110
53....300	275	7	56	7		106.....75	2	71	101	216
54....174	182	163	57	163		107......121	308	110	100	259
55....118	286	309	58	309		108......37	360	216	97	217
56....81-2	287	6	45	6		109.....138	165	259	99	308
57.... 215	183	79	46	79		110....348	249	217	84	165
58....291	228	275	52	275		111......230	83	2	103	249
59.... 172	—	182	344	182		112.....349	248	308	95	83
60.... 70	290	286	322	286		113.....341	201	165	96	248
61....292	198	287	345	287		114......34	202	249	114	201
62..... 93	173	183	48	183		115.....123	203	83	151	202
63....293	288	228	50	228		116.....169	204	248	133	203
64....260	289	290	324	198		117......35	205	201	111	204
65....120	279	198	54	173		118.....122	196	202	55	205
66....316	8	173	342	288		119......43	119	203	326	196
67.... 229	280	288	47	289		120.....281	218	204	127	119
68 ...109	108	289	321	279		121.....176	72	205	188	218
69....199	107	279	49	8		122.....184	73	196	115	72
70....164	310	8	40	290		123.....128	301	119	117	73
71..... 94	92	280	34	280		124...... 53	112	218	116	301
72.... 71	214	108	38	310		125.....185	294	72	125	112
73....110	69	107	43	92		126.....186	247	73	194	294
74....216	269	310	41	170		127.....187	358	301	148	247
75....259	297	92	42	80		128...... 10	200	112	149	200
76....217	299	214	53	143		129...... 9	111	294	150	111
77.... 1	144	69	51	269		130...... 41	328	247	155	328
78 308	300	269	36	214		131...... 40	281	200	154	281
79....165	174	297	37	69		132...... 42	359	111	153	168
80....249	118	299	11	107		133...... 11	168	328	161	342
81.... 83	81-2	300	323	108		134....241	342	281	160	44
82....248	215	144	64	297		135¹....129	44	168	159	209
83....218	291	81	135	299		136.... 12	209	44	103	36
84....251	70	81	136	144		137......188	—	209	167	75
85....201	172	174	137	300		138...... 38	36	36	166	121
86....202	292	118	138	174		139...... 54	75	75	190	122
87....203	293	215	139	118		140...... 95	121	121	168	37
88....204	93	291	140	81-2		141...... 96	122	122	186	138
89....205	260	70	44	215		142.....189	37	37	187	348
90....119	80	172	131	291		143.....351	138	138	169	230
91..... 36	143	292	74	172		144.....350	348	348	184	349
92....111	170	293	346	70		145.....254	—	230	178	1
93....112	—	93	122	292		146.....250	—	349	206	34
94....301	316	260	—	293		147......255	230	1	208	123
95..... 72	120	80	325	93		148.....256	349	34	207	74
96.... 73	229	143	132	260		149.....257	1	123	329	274
97....294	109	170	134	316		150.....258	34	74	175	43
98....247	199	316	130	120		151.....242	123	43	177	169
99....200	164	120	86	229		152......220	74	169	222	176

¹ W 135* = 157.

	Bl	B	W	M	Du
153	219	274	176	281	224
154	221	43	224	223	162
155	13	169	162	231	261
156	39	176	261	230	53
157	252	224	53	241	187
158	238	162	187	244	185
159	240	261	185	243	186
160	239	53	186	253	10
161	311	187	10	245	9
162	113	185	9	77	41
163	312	186	41	330	40
164	313	10	40	276	42
165	32	9	42	295	11
166	318	41	11	331	241
167	315	40	241	246	38
168	33	42	38	303	188
169	314	11	188	302	129
170	206	241	129	307	12
171	245	38	12	306	54
172	244	188	54	304	250
173	115	129	250	232	95
174	77	12	95	319	96
175	319	54	96	2	189
176	304	250	189	1	351
177	207	95	351	8	350
178	303	96	350	6	350
179	302	189	255	7	254
180	276	351	254	274	257
181	246	350	257	182	256
182	306	255	256	173	258
183	148	254	242	71	242
184	243	257	220	79	220
185	357	256	219	80	219
186	84	242	221	81	221
187	231	220	13	82	13
188	307	219	39	69	39
189	166	221	252	347	252
190	114	13	238	94	238
191	85	39	240	91	240
192	3	252	35	90	35
193	4	238	239	118	239
194	356	240	311	93	311
195	56	35	113	92	113
196	57	239	312	108	312
197	346	311	313	109	313
198	58	113	32	107	32
199	97	312	318	110	318
200	159	313	315	144	315
201	100	32	33	143	33
202	175	318	314	172	314
203	149	315	106	157	106
204	25	33	327	152	327
205	31	314	233	158	233
206	101	106	234	156	234
207	88	327	210	164	210
208	29	233	267	163	367

	Bl	B	W	M	Du
209	30	234	225	170	225
210	87	210	146	199	146
211	59	267	271	198	271
212	102	225	193	196	193
213	65	146	—	197	—
214	24	271	263	217	263
215	66	193	264	214	264
216	161	—	235	215	235
217	26	263	226	70	226
218	27	264	180	228	180
219	28	235	282	229	282
220	61	226	268	227	268
221	67	180	145	183	145
222	62	282	311	174	211
223	60	268	212	216	212
224	68	145	195	269	195
225	63	211	236	260	236
226	23	212	—	273	—
227	89	195	191	275	191
228	232	236	237	171	237
229	85	—	78	280	78
230	340	191	313	181	213
231	104	237	277	279	277
232	105	78	265	278	265
233	160	313	266	292	266
234	167	277	192	259	192
235	253	265	283	300	283
236	295	266	—	287	—
237	103	192	335	293	335
238	64	283	354	285	354
239	98	335	336	284	—
240	177	—	—	286	336
241	124	354	147	288	—
242	99	—	—	291	147
243	321	336	317	309	—
244	133	—	355	290	317
245	47	147	—	289	355
246	76	—	272	298	—
247	352	317	141	296	272
248	329	355	—	299	141
249	150	—·	179	120	—
250	151	272	337	305	179
251	155	141	—	297	337
252	5	—	—	308	—
253	262	179	—	310	—
254	353	337	—	316	206
255	125	—	—	13	245
256	330	—	—	113	244
257	208	222	—	39	77
258	153	262	222	32	319
259	326	190	262	33	251
260	14	48	190	73	304
261	126	208	48	72	303
262	222	131	—	83	302
263	322	51	208	119	276
264	52	246	131	112	264

	Bl	B	W	M	Du
265	15	178	51	165	306
266	16	84	246	142	148
267	51	270	178	162	243
268	190	153	84	219	84
269	154	148	270	209	231
270	131	251	153	328	307
271	178	206	148	200	166
272	17	276	251	202	114
273	18	304	206	203	222
274	19	303	276	204	262
275	45	302	304	205	190
276	46	306	303	349	48
277	345	245	302	224	208
278	324	244	306	239	131
279	344	114	245	238	51
280	132	231	244	240	178
281	48	166	114	221	270
282	20	77	231	220	153
283	21	319	166	242	115
284	50	307	77	252	117
285	22	243	319	218	116
286	194	115	307	248	125
287	270	117	243	250	194
288	117	116	115	247	22
289	116	125	117	179	17
290	136	194	116	261	18
291	140	22	125	251	19
292	137	17	194	35	325
293	139	18	22	201	345
294	127	19	17	294	45
295	332	—	19	301	55
296	323	325	325	249	140
297	343	345	345	313	—
298	49	45	45	312	323
299	134	55	55	311	139
300	325	140	140	314	15
301	130	—	—	315	326
302	55	323	323	318	127
303	320	139	139	327	52
304	338	15	15	210	322
305	339	326	326	213	21
306	333	127	127	211	207
307	334	52	52	212	14
308	135	322	18	78	324
309	106	21	322	225	154
310	327	207	21	226	344
311	233	14	207	234	50
312	234	324	14	237	49
313	210	154	324	233	341
314	267	344	154	236	16
315	225	50	344	235	343
316	146	27	50	191	332
317	271	49	49	268	46
318	263	341	341	192	20
319	264	68	16	145	130
320	235	26	343	146	134

	Bl	B	W	M	Du
321	226	16	332	264	353
322	180	343	46	265	330
323	282	332	20	266	—
324	268	46	130	195	137
325	145	20	134	263	136
326	212	130	353	277	126
327	211	134	330	180	132
328	195	—	—	282	—
329	236	353	137	267	97
330	191	330	136	▬	98
331	237	—	126		159
332	78	89	132		57
333	213	137	—		346
334	277	136	333		99
335	265	126	—		100
336	216	67	334		58
337	192	132	97		56
338	283	340	159		133
339	272 / 335	—	57		85
340	354	97	346		3
341	336	98	99		4
342	147	159	100		356
343	317	57	58		47
344	355	346	56		177
345	141	99	133		124
346	179	—	85		321
347	337	100	3		175
348	331	58	4		76
349	223	56	47		352
350	224	133	177		329
351	142	85	124		103
352	162	3	321		331
353	261	356	175		150
354	▬	4	76		135
355		177	352		151
356		177	329		155
357		124	103		184
358		321	331		64
359		175	150		142
360		76	135		223
361		352	151		128
362		329	155		320
363		103	184		5
364		331	64		▬
365		150	143		
366		135	223		
367		151	128		
368		155	320		
369		184	5		
370		64	▬		
371		142			
372		223			
373		128			
374		320			
375		5			

.